ALWAYS
UP FRONT

$\mathcal{A}$LWAYS UP FRONT

THE MEMOIRS OF
HELEN FRIED KIRSHBLUM GOLDSTEIN
AS TOLD TO
MYRNA KATZ FROMMER

To Sandy & Leo
Best wishes to our
fellow congregants
Myrna Katz Frommer

gefen גפן
publishing house בית הוצאה לאור
JERUSALEM ◆ NEW YORK

The painting "*Supreme Court, Jerusalem*"
(*oil on canvas*, 1994) is courtesy of the painter Paul Benney.

Typesetting: Jerusalem Typesetting, Jerusalem

ISBN 965-229-338-5

1   3   5   7   9   8   6   4   2

Gefen Publishing House	Gefen Books
6 Hatzvi Street, Jerusalem 94386, Israel	600 Broadway, Lynbrook, NY 11563, USA
972-2-538-0247 • orders@gefenpublishing.com	1-800-477-5257 • orders@gefenpublishing.com

www.israelbooks.com

Printed in Israel   *Send for our free catalogue*

To my grandparents: Isaac and Anna Boehm z"l, my father and mother: Joseph and Rose Feiner z"l, my husbands: Albert Fried z"l, Rabbi I. Usher Kirshblum z"l, and Rabbi Leonard J. Goldstein.

To my sons: Arthur and Michael, my daughters-in-law: Susan and Janet, and my nine grandchildren.

To my five great-grandchildren and my great-grandchildren yet to be born. I pray they will carry forth the ideals and live by the values of their grandparents and their great-grandfather, Albert Fried z"l.

CONTENTS

INTRODUCTION

THE IDEA FOR THIS BOOK first emerged in the midst of rehabilitation therapy that followed the stroke I suffered several years ago. At that time, Dr. Judith Leventhal of the Rusk Institute asked me to bring in some photos of my past, and I began sharing with her the events they prompted me to recall. It was then that she suggested I write the story of my life.

"Who would be interested?" I asked. The thought of writing an auto-biography had never before crossed my mind.

"Well, I think not only your family and friends but even strangers. You've led such a remarkable life," she said.

Thus were the seeds for this book planted. But they would have remained dormant if not for a family discussion around the *Shabbat* table of my children Michael and Janet. As usual, I was telling a story of one of my experiences when my granddaughter Miriam piped up, "Nanny, you've had such an exciting and productive life. Why don't you write a book?"

Whereupon my husband Leonard responded, "We have already explored that possibility and found it too expensive." Indeed, Leonard's dearest and long-time friend Mel Kirzon had tried to get the project off the ground some months earlier only to find the cost prohibitive.

Without a moment's hesitation, Michael said, "Mom, forget about the expenses. I'll take care of them. Do it." And at that moment, the seeds took root.

There was never any doubt about whom I wanted to work with me in the creation of this autobiography. From the moment our eyes met in the office we shared at Kingsborough Community College of the City University of New York, I knew Myrna and I were going to be friends. She was young enough to be my daughter, one of those daughters I always wanted. Yet the age difference didn't matter. Attractive and sophisticated-looking, she scored high on my antennae scale.

Over the years I followed Myrna's writing career, read her many articles on Jewish communities around the world and her books of oral histories that contain some of my own stories. I knew she had the talent and *neshama* to make of the events of my life a true and meaningful tale.

And I was not wrong. Our working together has been joyous at times, painful at others, but always a creative adventure marked by mutual affection and esteem.

My gratitude to Myrna extends to her husband, Harvey, a popular sports writer and oral historian, who read the evolving manuscript and provided invaluable feedback.

It extends tenfold to my husband. Leonard, who in the generosity that has characterized our life together, printed up chapter after chapter that were sent via e-mail so I could read them, and when my eyes grew tired, read to me. He guided the process from start to finish, offering suggestions, providing information, finding and dealing with a publisher, and being there for each of the steps that brought this work from rough manuscript to final copy with the utmost attentiveness and devotion.

And my gratitude extends to Leonard's son Michael C. Goldstein as well, who took on the exacting and time-consuming task of copy-editing and fact checking with a willingness, competence, and intelligence that matched his father's.

I concluded this book with some reluctance. Events piled on events and asked for inclusion. Since the manuscript that became this book went on its way to publication, my granddaughter Alissa gave birth to my first great-grandson, Yonatan, and my granddaughter Abigail gave birth to my fourth great-granddaughter, Libi. At the same time, my granddaughter Miriam passed the New York State bar exam. They are part of this story too.

There are others who are part of this story, individuals most dear to me, who because of the narrative structure of this memoir, are not mentioned in the pages that follow. I list them here in gratitude for their friendship, devotion, and having enriched my life immeasurably.

Annabelle Argand, Edya Arzt *z"l*, Evelyn Auerbach, Carolyn Baron, Gloria B. Cohen, Audrey Citak, Tom Curley, Rabbi Carol Davidson, Rabbi Moshe *z"l* and Lottie Davis, Mitzi Eisenberg, Dr. Mark Fromer, Lila Frost, Anita Gluck, Phyllis Haas, Michael Katz and Ellie Henkind Katz, Gerson and Carol Kekst, Rabbi Charles L. Klein, Goldie Kweller *z"l*, Eitan and Rachel Lev, Dr. Edward Lipke, Rabbi Morris Margolies, Hadassah Nadich, Ruth Perry, Arnold and Dawn Pohl, Claire Jacobson Quittman, Dr. Leon Pachter, Selma Rapaport Pressman, Robert de Rothschild, Fran Schuloff, Ethel Schwartz, Evelyn Seelig, Rabbi Reuven Siegel, Stanley and Charlotte Silber, Marion Siner *z"l*, Rabbi David Small, Rabbi Yaakov and Sarah Thompson, Janet Tobin, Rabbi Isaac and Fran Trainin, Dr. Marcel Tuchman, Pamella Tyndall, Henry Vorenberg, Judge Moses Weinstein, Morris (Tiny) Weintraub *z"l* and Selma Weintraub, Fred and Harriet Winter, Judy Yudof, Sumner and Hortense Zabriski, Professor Dr. Josef Zander.

Writing this book has been both exhilarating and wrenching. At the age of ninety-one, I can look back on a long life and say it was good. I am grateful to God for the many gifts bestowed on me and for allowing me, in some small measure, to contribute to *Tikkun Olam*.

Helen Fried Kirshblum Goldstein
New York, New York.
Fall, 2003

PREFACE

Helen and i began work on her life story last February, one month shy of her ninety-first birthday. We quickly settled on a routine. I'd show up at her apartment with my tape recorder at 8:30 in the morning, and for the next two hours I'd ask her questions and she'd tell me stories. A rather early start but it couldn't be helped. The rest of her day was already taken up. Invariably there was a development meeting at the Jewish Theological Seminary, a board meeting of the Jewish Braille Institute, a planning session for a Women's League for Conservative Judaism function, a lecture she had to hear, an exhibition she had to see, a luncheon she had to attend.

But for those two early morning hours, Helen was all mine. The front door would be ajar. I'd let myself in and there she'd be waiting for me, red hair perfectly coiffed, makeup complete, wearing a rose-colored satin robe and a welcoming smile. We'd begin.

Many of her stories were already familiar to me as Helen and I had been friends for more than twenty years. I can still remember the day we met. I was a new professor at Kingsborough Community College and had entered the office I was assigned to share with a senior professor. There I was greeted by a wall of photographs, all of well-known figures, people like Nelson Rockefeller, Earl Warren, Robert F. Kennedy, David Ben-Gurion, Elie Wiesel. And beside each of them was an attractive woman wearing a pill box hat entirely covered with lilac blossoms.

A few minutes later, the woman in the photographs sailed into the office. She was still wearing a hat, only this one looked like something out of *Gone with the Wind*, an appropriate accessory for the woman our chairman, Dr. Mortimer Becker *z"l*, used to call "the Scarlett O'Hara of the Speech Department."

His soubriquet for Helen was, in some respects, on the mark. Like Scarlett O'Hara, Helen is brave and determined, optimistic and confident. And she shares the quintessential southern belle's take-charge attitude. Where was I from, she now demanded to know. What courses was I teaching? What was my family like? My responses must have led her to assume I was Jewish because her next question was, what synagogue did I belong to? And that response brought a smile of recognition. She knew the temple; she knew the rabbi. A few weeks later, when I told the rabbi about my meeting Helen, he told me about the time he was standing on a staircase and was so distracted watching her walk up, he nearly lost his footing. Helen could have such an effect on people – even rabbis.

Although we were a generation apart, we became close confidantes. We shared a love of teaching, a belief in the importance of communication skills, an interest in Jewish affairs, and also a fondness for fashion – somewhat of an anomaly in our academic environs. We would get together for coffee in between classes, we socialized outside of school. She encouraged me to pursue a doctorate and kept tabs on my progress. And she maintained the connection between us even after we were no longer teaching colleagues.

So the material of Helen's life was familiar to me and our friendship was a given. But as we plunged into the depths of her past and she courageously confronted times of pain and loss as well as joy and achievement, our relationship deepened. Also I began to see her life as it played out against the backdrop of larger world events and how she was simultaneously a woman of her time and a woman ahead of her time – the living embodiment of the old adage: "If you want something done, give it to a busy woman."

At the end of our two-hour sessions, Helen would walk me to the elevator, and I would leave in a mood of serenity and contentment, a state of being that remained unarticulated, even unexamined, until the day our conversation turned to a concern of my own. Ever interested and empathetic, Helen pursued the subject. But we had much work ahead of us and no time to spare. "I don't want to bother you with my *tsuris*," I said to her.

"But your *tsuris* is my *tsuris*," Helen said to me.

And at that moment, the feeling that had been hovering about me over the past months came into focus. During our hours together, I had been the recipient of a supportive, non-judgmental affection bathed in an aura of *Yiddishkeit* with all that implies, which had been part of the very air I breathed until my mother died more than fourteen years ago. I did not know how much I missed it until now.

Appropriately our journey ends at the start of the Jewish New Year, a time for endings as well as beginnings. I move on with some reluctance. Now that our regular encounters are over, the unexpected gift Helen gave me cannot be expected to continue. But it abides within me, a treasured memory, radiant as a rose-colored satin robe.

Myrna Katz Frommer
Lyme, New Hampshire
Fall, 2003

PART ONE

I

PORT CHESTER

I WAS BORN on a cold and snowy March day in 1912, on the big oval-shaped table that stood in the center of our dining room. My big brother, Hy, and little sister, Nettie, were born there as well. In years to come, we would have our meals and do our homework around that table. It was where we'd celebrate birthdays and holidays, entertain company, and be together as a family. That dining room table was the heart of my childhood home.

We lived in Port Chester, a small, peaceful town in Westchester County, where New York State meets Connecticut. My father's family, the Feiners, were very prominent in Port Chester. How they got there, I don't know. Probably my father's sister, Tante Deena, came first. She was the oldest one. Others must have followed.

We lived in a three-story multiple-family house on Purdy Avenue, a side street that fell into a dirt road. There were no sidewalks, but the road was lined with maple and sycamore trees that cast deep shadows across the byway. Few cars were around then; horses and wagons came up and down Purdy Avenue all day long. I can still hear the clippity-clop of the horse that drew the milkman's wagon early every morning and the ice wagon that carried those big blocks of ice.

To get anywhere, we had to take the trolley on Main Street, a few blocks away. Or we'd cut through the back lots that ran behind our house. In the spring and summer, the lots were filled with perennials, changing as the seasons moved along. We'd pick daisies and wind them into yellow

3

crowns for our hair or play "He loves me/he loves me not," tearing off a petal as we thought of the person we cared about.

In the summers, Mama would take us to Rye Beach. We went back and forth on the trolley, and on the way home, she'd buy each of us an ice cream cone. They cost a nickel apiece back then. I was a very slow eater, especially with something I enjoyed, and would still be licking my ice cream cone after my brother and sister had finished theirs. They'd be looking at me imploringly, and sometimes I let them have a lick. But I was in control, having managed to make mine last the whole journey.

Our house was far from the biggest or the most beautiful house on Purdy Avenue, but it had nice yards in the front and back, and a stoop where we congregated and played stoopball. There were four apartments on each floor, and a single toilet in the hall on the first floor. Thankfully, our apartment was on the first floor.

My best friend, Maria, was a little Italian girl who also lived on the first floor. She was so pretty with a wonderful smile and long dark hair. We always played together and shared our dolls. Then, when she was around five years old, she came down with diphtheria and died. It happened very fast. I was absolutely devastated; it was my first experience with death.

About two weeks later, I saw one of Maria's dolls, a soft and cuddly rag doll with blonde curls, in the trash container that had been put out to be collected. I rescued it from the trash and pressed it to my heart.

Soon afterwards, Maria's mother saw me playing with the doll. She ran over and grabbed it out of my hands. "This doesn't belong to you. It belongs to Maria," she cried. I felt terrible. I didn't understand what I had done that was wrong.

Our neighborhood was very mixed: Jews, Italians, and Irish. I never noticed any anti-Semitism, but there were differences. Tante Chana Blima's husband, Joe Friedenberg, was a very well-to-do tailor in Port Chester who always drove a late model car. One day, his next-door neighbor, Charlie Flanagan, stopped him and said, "Joe, how can you afford to get a new car all the time?"

My uncle turned to him and said, "Charlie, do you smoke?"

"Yeah, I smoke cigars."

My uncle asked, "Do you play cards?"

"Sure, I play poker at least once a week."

"How about drinking?"

"Well, I generally drop in at the bar and have a few with the guys."

"Well, Charlie," said my uncle Joe, "I don't smoke, I don't play cards, and I don't drink. That's how I can afford to buy a new car."

Although we didn't have a car, my father, Joseph, did have a horse. Nellie was part of the family. She stayed in a wooden barn right next door to our house, and we adored her. Once, she kicked me while I was playing with her, and they had to rush me to the hospital. But that didn't get in the way of my loving Nellie. I felt it was my fault; I must have done something that made her kick me.

My father was what some people might call a junk-peddler. His two fixed assets were Nellie and a wooden wagon. Very early every morning, he'd set out for the wealthy neighborhoods of Port Chester, Rye, Mamaroneck, and Larchmont, where he would go door-to-door buying furnishings, decorative items, and bric-a-brac. Then he'd turn around and try to sell them.

I had this tremendous love for my father, and being a peddler didn't seem to me to be good enough for him. Although looking back on it now, I realize he was actually an antique dealer who bought and sold some very valuable objects. Once, he brought home a brass candlelit chandelier. It was magnificent, much too elaborate for our home. He sold it quickly, but I remember hoping we would be able to keep it.

In addition to the dining room, our apartment had a big kitchen and four bedrooms. One bedroom was for Mama and Papa, one was for Nettie and me, one was for Hy, and the remaining bedroom was reserved for whomever happened to have come over from Poland or Russia around that time. There were always new immigrants who stayed with us until they were able to get a job and take care of themselves. What I remember most about these people is how they smelled; they had a certain soap-smell that I found very attractive. I used to think how wonderful it was that these people had traveled so far and still they had this wonderful smell.

Both my parents were immigrants from Poland or Russia – the borders were shifting then. My mother's family, the Boehms, came from Lodz, my father's from a little shtetl called Neustadt, which means New Town.

When my father came to America before the First World War, he had left his pregnant wife behind. His plan was to get settled and then bring her and the baby over. However, she died in childbirth, and the baby, Chaneleh, was taken by her maternal grandmother and raised in Neustadt.

Twice during the First World War, Papa sent money for Chaneleh to come here, but it never reached her. The third time he found someone to deliver the money personally. Then, at last, Chaneleh came over and met her father. She was seventeen years old by this time, and the transition was very difficult for her. She couldn't mix well with us. She didn't speak English. But we managed; we loved her because she was a loveable person.

My mother, Rose, was a beautiful woman and from a very good family. The Boehms had been very well educated in Europe, and here they became quite wealthy. My grandfather, Isaac Boehm, was *gabbai* of one of the first Conservative synagogues in Brooklyn.

I always felt my mother married down. My father wasn't such a catch. He had a child in Europe that he had to bring here. He was regarded as a peddler, which wasn't such a prestigious occupation. But when my mother was about eighteen, she lost all her hair. No one knew why it happened. Her scalp became absolutely bare. It was around that time that she met my father. She was a smart girl, high spirited. She knew what she wanted and would go for it. And what she wanted was to get married and have a family. She wasn't about to let the fact that she didn't have any hair stop her.

After they got married, my parents moved to Port Chester to be near his family. Even though my father was on a different level from most of the Feiners because he was a peddler, I don't think he felt bad about it because there was so much love in that family. It was a fun-loving, happy family – different from my mother's, which was colder and much more serious.

I never knew anyone in the Feiner family who was angry at anyone, and I never heard Papa say a bad word about anybody. Later on in life, I realized he did not like Mama's sister Fannie, who was kind of a sad sack. Still, he was good to her, included her in everything, and did not let on how he felt about her.

He was gentle, never harsh. I never heard him raise his voice. He seemed to love the whole world. I loved my father so much, more than my mother. And I felt sorry for him, because I had the impression that my mother did not enjoy sex. I always pictured her saying, "No, no, no."

Mama was the disciplinarian in the family; she was very firm, even severe. We had to all sit down and eat together – except for Papa if he were late because of work. She was very fastidious. Everything had to be so clean and neat; the house had to be spic and span.

Her door was open to anyone who came for a handout. I remember the religious Jews in particular, because they looked different. But she never questioned any of them. All got money. The windowsill was lined with *tzedakah* boxes from ever so many places. She would drop coins in on Fridays before lighting candles if something good happened, if there was a problem that had to be overcome, or for no apparent reason at all.

And Mama used to do *bikkur cholim*, visiting the sick and homebound, which is a *mitzvah*. She would schlep me along, not my brother or sister, just me. In the beginning I didn't want to go. But after a while, I began to appreciate it. Once, we visited a woman who had her own private room in a nursing home. Mother opened the door and quickly shut it.

"What is it, Mama?" I asked.

"Oh my God," she said, "Mary is in bed with a man!"

When I came home from school on Friday, I had to scrub the kitchen floor. It was an easy job, because with my mother around, it never got dirty. I would have liked a little more of a challenge. Then Mama would fill our cast-iron tub with water that she heated up on the big black stove, and each of us would take a bath. When we were done, the white chairs that sat around the kitchen table would go into the tub. I used to think Mama was much too clean.

Because Papa had to work on *Shabbos*, we did not go to synagogue. But Friday night was Friday night. Mama lit the candles, Papa made the blessing over the wine and *challah* that Mama had baked. She loved to fix *Shabbos* dinner, the chicken soup with little yellow chicken eggs, the gefilte fish, the chicken, and potato *kugel*.

She also made a *cholent* for Saturday lunch when we couldn't light the stove. All Friday night, it would simmer in a very low oven. We could smell the meat, the potatoes, and beans cooking with the bones that the butcher threw in for nothing. What an aroma!

On *Shabbos*, Mama would take us on a long walk to one of our aunts' houses. All of these ladies were marvelous bakers, and they competed with one another in making beautiful complicated cakes: sweet layer cakes, strawberry shortcakes, the kinds kids really like. My mother didn't compete with them; she probably felt that she wasn't in their league. She stuck to her specialty – a *babka*, which was a kind of cinnamon-nut cake. It may have been simple to make, but it was delicious.

When it came to sewing, however, Mama's creations were hardly simple. She sewed most of our clothes, and some things, like the plaid pleated skirts she made for Nettie and me, were quite complicated. The sewing machine sat in my parents' bedroom, and we were forbidden to go near it. But I developed a fascination with sewing from my earliest days, and I often would sneak in and play with it. One day, the needle of the machine went through my finger, and I had to be rushed to the hospital.

I was always into everything, very extroverted. Nettie may have been prettier than I, with her curly hair that Mother would make into long ringlets, but that didn't bother me. I loved her. If anything, I think I probably stymied Nettie as a child because I was so bubbly. She was quieter and not too good a student.

Hy, on the other hand, was very scholarly, very smart. I could never do math, and Hy would help me with my homework. He'd scream at me until I'd say, "I don't want you to help me anymore." He would go away, then come back and try to help me again. He was also very athletic. I remember him putting on shorts and setting out to run on the streets. "What are you doing, *meshuggina*?" Mama would cry after him.

When my brother started kindergarten, I begged my mother to take me along with him. The teacher said I was too young and wouldn't admit me. I cried all the way home. "That's it," Mama said. "You'll have to wait until next year to start school."

But the next morning, I got up, dressed myself, and followed Hy to school. I sat down quietly in the back of the class. For a few days, I just kept returning and sitting in the back. The teacher, who had beautiful hair with long curls flowing down her back, didn't say anything to me, but by the fourth day, I was accepted as a student. Immediately, I moved up front to a seat in the first row.

I always wanted to do what my brother did, so a few years later, when Hy started Hebrew school, I followed him once again. He went to a typical *Talmud Torah* in the only synagogue in Port Chester, an Orthodox *shul* in a most unsubstantial building. It wasn't until I moved to Brooklyn that I realized a synagogue is more than just a storefront.

This time I didn't get past the front door when I heard, "Wshhhh! Get out, kid!" Rabbi Ginsburg wasn't even nice. I was tenacious; I tried it over and over again, but it was always, "Out you go!" That was because I was a girl. I went back and told my parents. But they just sloshed it off. There was nothing for girls in Jewish education back then.

I fared better with piano lessons, which I took on Tante Malke's upright piano. Her kids wouldn't take lessons, and she loved me. So she felt very good about my taking lessons and practicing at her house. As for me, I not only took to the piano immediately, I loved to go to Tante Malke's house. She was the best baker in the family, and in addition to playing the piano, I always got a plateful of cookies.

To get to Tante Malke's house, I used to cut through the lots to King Street, where she lived. She had a much fancier house than ours in a much wealthier neighborhood. So did Tante Chana Blima, whose house had one of those big wide porches.

My life in Port Chester was dominated by the Feiner family. They were all so warm and loving, and our times were filled with getting together and having good times, especially for birthdays, anniversaries, and holidays.

Although the Feiners accepted my mother with much love, and although they were a well-known family and very involved in the community of Port Chester, I think Mama secretly longed to be closer to her family. She must have had that desire in her heart for a long time. But it wasn't until I was about thirteen years old that she broached the subject of our moving to my father.

I don't know how she talked him into it. She was a sharp lady and knew when to say something and how to say it. So she must have waited for the right moment. I can just picture her sitting him down one day when he came home from work and saying, "Yusell, under no circumstances would I ever want to leave Port Chester and your family. But you know that Jewish boys in Port Chester are not dating the Jewish girls. Or, if they are, they're dating the richer girls from New Rochelle and Mamaroneck. Our girls will never find fellas here. That's a serious thing. I think we've got to get out."

When the news was broken to us, it was such a surprise. We never expected it. We cried. We didn't want to leave. We had enjoyed taking the commuter train to Grand Central – even though I always got sick on that train – and then going by trolley into Brooklyn. But it was devastating to sell Nellie, to leave Port Chester and all our friends, and the cousins and aunts to whom we were so attached. My entire world was in Port Chester.

Mama got her wish, however, and before the year was out we had moved to Brooklyn. I got to know the Boehm family very well and love them as much as the Feiners. And Mama was right. It was a good move for all of us. But because of all the years in Port Chester, the warmth of the Feiners had seeped into me, become part of me. It would stay with me forever.

II

BROOKLYN

Moving from port chester to Brooklyn was like moving from the country to the city. I missed the open spaces. I missed Nellie and all my friends. Most of all though, I missed the Feiner family. There was such a closeness; we were like one solid piece. But then again, my mother's family – her parents, Isaac and Anna Boehm, her brother, Sam, her sister Fannie, and their families – all received us so well. Mother had another sister, Gussie, who had moved to Cleveland, Ohio, with her husband, but they came to visit often.

The focus now became the Boehm family. My grandparents had come to this country when their children were in their late teens. My grandfather had some money and opened up a printing press. That led to his establishing the Philosophical Press together with my Uncle Sam – the youngest of the children and Grandfather's favorite. They published philosophical and biographical books.

Our first year in Brooklyn we lived with my grandparents while my parents looked around for a suitable apartment. Their home was in Bay Ridge, an elegant neighborhood, and not exclusively Jewish; there were Swedes and Norwegians as well, many of them important families. My grandparents' house was a brownstone. You could enter either from the street level into the lower floor, or up a flight of exterior steps that led to a set of large double doors. Beyond was the living room with its magnificent Tiffany chandelier.

The Boehm style of living was different from the Feiners'. For my Port

11

Chester aunts, the focus had been on food. For my Grandma Anna, although she was a wonderful cook, the focus was on the table: the fine silver, the beautiful porcelain dishes, and the hand-embroidered tablecloths.

Grandma was a pretty and petite woman with such tiny feet that her shoes and bedroom slippers looked like they were made for a doll. She was gentle and quiet. I never heard her raise her voice. Not that she could with Grandpa around. He ruled that family. The children were intimidated by him, and I guess she was, as well. He was always very loving and playful with me, but he could be stern.

A handsome gentleman of a good height, Grandpa was the spokesperson for the Bay Ridge Jewish community. His house was always filled with people: synagogue members, owners of the shops on Fourth Avenue, and students from the Jewish Theological Seminary, who stayed over *Shabbat* to study with rabbis and cantors. My grandfather's living room was like a salon.

Isaac Boehm was a lay person, but the most important lay person in the congregation of B'nai Israel. As soon as you walked into the synagogue lobby, you faced a painting of him hanging on the wall. Seeing it always made me feel so good and proud.

We went to his Conservative synagogue now for the High Holy Days, and I was struck by the great difference between B'nai Israel and the little Orthodox *shul* we used to attend in Port Chester. This synagogue must have been built some time in the late nineteenth century. It was a beautiful building with exquisite stained glass windows. Its atmosphere was austere yet heartwarming. Everyone was orderly and composed.

My grandfather would be up there on the *bimah*, the silver threads on the neck of his *tallit* glittering as he stood before the *Torahs* that were draped in embroidered velvet mantles. When they lifted the *Torahs*, the little ornaments on top of the scrolls would tinkle. It was like a fantasy world to me.

Now that we were living in Brooklyn, my father began to work for his younger brother, Max, who owned a factory in nearby Borough Park. It was a very successful concern. Uncle Max made a lot of money. His wife, Aunt Annie, was the only one I knew who had domestic help.

His company knitted cloth that was sold to clothing manufacturers; he also manufactured women's clothes for fancy department stores like Saks Fifth Avenue and Bonwit Teller. His knitting machines were very complicated, and since Papa was very mechanical, he could take a machine apart, fix it, and put it back together again – he became quite an asset to Uncle Max.

Uncle Max took my father into his business as a worker, not as a partner, which always bothered me. At first, he didn't pay him very much. Still, working for his brother, Papa earned more than he had with Nellie and the wagon up in Port Chester.

One day Papa came home and told us that Max had bought himself a beautiful new watch. "What did he do with his old watch?" Mama asked.

Papa had the saddest look on his face. "I asked him for it, and he refused to give it to me," he said.

Well, if I had my Uncle Max in that room, I would have choked him. What did he need another watch for, I said to myself. His other wrist?

Mama took me to register at the local school. They tested me and decided to place me in a program called the RA for rapid advance, where you completed the seventh and eighth grades in one year. At the beginning of the term, I had trouble understanding the other kids' speech. They spoke in what I later learned was called Brooklynese. What a lovely way to speak, I thought. I tried to mimic them, and one day I told my teacher, "I'm trying to learn to speak like everyone else, but I'm having a hard time."

She said to me, "My dear Helen, I am looking forward to everyone in the class speaking just like you."

After a year or so, we moved into an apartment on Forty-sixth Street, between Fifth and Sixth Avenues. I settled in quickly and made friends with the kids in the neighborhood. It was a hilly area, and one winter there was a great deal of snow. They didn't clear it for weeks, and it was piled up high on the sides of the streets. We all had sleds, some big enough for several kids, and we would toboggan down the big hill on Forty-fifth Street from Seventh to Fourth Avenues. At the bottom of each street, we posted a monitor to watch the traffic. He'd signal if the coast was clear or if we had to get over to the ash pile and wait for the cars to pass.

Even though the hill continued beyond Fourth Avenue, that's where we would stop, because we had to carry the sleds all the way uphill. We were a crowd of kids from different ethnic groups, all friends, playing outdoors in the cold brisk air. It felt so healthy and invigorating, unless Andy, a very fat kid, was on your sled. We bellied down, one kid lying on top of the other. No one wanted to be under Andy.

Music remained an important part of the Feiner family life. Hy, who had been studying the violin since he was a small boy, continued with his lessons, and I kept up with the piano. Only now we had our own piano so I could practice at home. I did have to go to the teacher's house for my lessons, and Mama would give me a couple of nickels to take the trolley back and forth. But I would sneak my roller skates out of the house and skate all the way instead. How many times I would come to my piano teacher all out of breath and with scraped knees. But what a great trip, so free and out in the open. As for the nickels Mama gave me, I'd squirrel them away. That was the beginning of my squirreling away money, something I continued to do for much of my life.

My parents soon decided they wanted to live in a more Jewish neighborhood, so we moved to Bensonhurst. Our apartment was the lower floor of a semi-attached two-family house on Seventy-second Street, off of Bay Parkway. Aunt Fannie lived nearby. She was the *farbissina* in the family because of her unhappy marriage. Her husband was an intellectual; I remember him always reading. They had one son, Herman, who used to bother me to play with him. But I didn't like playing with Herman because he wanted to touch. Even though he was a good-looking kid, there was something about him I found distasteful.

About half a mile away, along Bay Parkway, was the JCH – the Jewish community center. I joined their theater group and enthusiastically did anything I was asked to do. I almost lived there. My mother was angry; she thought I was spending too much time at the JCH and not enough on my schoolwork. She was probably right. But I wanted so much to get a part in a play. I have always wanted to be on center stage.

On the way home from school, we would often stop by the candy store on Bay Parkway for a charlotte russe. That's a traditional Brooklyn confection – a little cake in a cardboard circle beneath a swirl of whipped cream, topped with a cherry. Once, a box of a dozen charlotte russes was set in the window of the candy store. I pressed my nose against the window longingly. "I could eat every one," I said to my friend. A big burly cab driver happened to be standing near us and overheard me. "Come on kid," he said. "You couldn't eat all of them."

"Oh yes I could."

"I'll bet you a dollar you can't eat all of them."

That was tempting. A dollar was a lot of money. "But who's going to pay for them?" I asked.

"I will."

I walked into the candy store, picked up the box and plunged in. What a treat! But by the time I got to the eighth one, I was feeling sick. I managed to finish them by shoving them into my face. And then I ran down to the curb and threw up.

The cabbie came over to me. "I'm not giving you a dollar, and I'm not even going to pay for the charlotte russes. You're a big phony. You didn't really eat them."

But the owner of the candy store, who was my friend and was just as burly as the cabbie, came out onto the sidewalk. "Come on, get off that," he said. "You're going to give her a dollar and pay for all those cakes to boot."

He did. I got the dollar. But never again have I eaten another charlotte russe.

They used to call me Chana Pessel, a character in the Yiddish theater who was always getting in and out of trouble, and getting others in and out of trouble as well. I couldn't refuse a dare.

Once, we were in Coney Island at some kind of parade where everyone was throwing confetti. When I came home, I found my mother all upset. "A terrible thing happened," she said. "I just heard from the police station. Hy is being held there."

"For what?" I asked.

"I don't know."

"Don't worry," I said, "I'll go down there and bring him home."

So this thirteen-year-old kid goes to the police station. "What has my brother done?" I asked. It turned out he and some friends had thrown some confetti into a girl's blouse.

"Please," I begged, "let my brother go home. He's a good kid. He was just fooling around. It was the spirit of the night. Please let him go."

I pleaded so hard that they finally relented and let my big brother go under his kid sister's care. That became a big family story.

When I was about fifteen, Aunt Hannah came into our lives. I had never heard of her until the day a letter arrived from Australia. That was the first time my father mentioned his sister who had run off with a gentile officer when she was sixteen. My grandparents must have wiped her off after that.

No one had heard from her all these years, but now she was writing, she said, because her husband died and she wanted to be in touch with her family once again. She packed up a trunk and sent it to us. How thrilled we were to open it and find the most extraordinary things, including an oil portrait of this very well-dressed woman with perfect carriage.

Soon after, Hannah came to New York and moved in with us. At that time, she must have been in her early fifties. The Feiners all welcomed her warmly, and though she was so totally different from anyone else in the family, she seemed to fit right in.

Aunt Hannah was tall, much taller than I expected, since most of my father's family was on the short side. I wouldn't say she was actually pretty, but she was elegant, and her example was unique in my life at that point. I had never seen such beautiful clothes and jewelry before. She also smelled so good, so different from anyone I knew, I imagine from the soaps or expensive perfumes she used. And she spoke with the most perfect British accent. Sometimes I think my interest in public speaking was spurred by the example set by Aunt Hannah.

She told us she had two children but they had died. Somehow we always thought that was a fiction. How could she move from one place to another with children? She had lived in India for many years before moving to Australia. The family thought her stories about life in India were fiction as well. But as I got to know more about the time of the British rule in India, I realized that her descriptions of the servants she had, the soldiers, and the teeming population were probably true. We kids would sit on the floor, listening to her tales, absolutely enchanted. She was like a fairy from another world.

Once she got settled, Aunt Hannah decided she was tired of doing nothing and was going to open up a kosher restaurant – even though she didn't remember much about kosher food. And that was exactly what she did.

She had money enough to set up this restaurant on Fourth Avenue above one of the stores. She decorated the room beautifully with plants all around and fine linens on the tables. It was a dairy restaurant, open for lunch and also for early dinners a few nights a week. The word got out quickly, and it was a big success. Aunt Hannah did all the cooking and baking herself, and she was a superb cook. As far as I can remember, she had only one person to help serve.

My grandfather Isaac Boehm as a young man. He was the inspiration for my involvement with Conservative Judaism

My parents
Rose and Joseph Feiner

I was always interested in fashion and knew how to put myself together, c.1930

Once Al and I started dating, I stopped seeing
everyone else. This picture was taken shortly
before our wedding in 1935

With Al Fried, Arthur and Michael on the stoop of our
Marine Park house, c. 1950

With Charlotte Levine. We met as young mothers in Marine
Park and have remained close friends ever since

Al Fried and I out on the town, 1952

With Rabbi Louis Finkelstein, Chancellor of the Jewish
Theological Seminary, some time in the early 1960's

The culminating event of the 1965
Women's League convention in
Jerusalem was the presentation of
the first Mathilde Schechter Award
to Golda Meir

Al Fried and I with Israel's President
Levi Eshkol in Jerusalem, 1965

With Yitzhak Rabin, 1965

With Robert F. Kennedy whose commitment to the
civil rights movement I admired, c.1965

With Roy Wilkins, director
of the Urban League, at the
White House Conference on
Civil Rights in 1966

Al Fried and I with
Chief Justice Earl
Warren in 1966

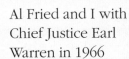

Al Fried and I with United Nations Ambassador
Arthur Goldberg, 1966

With a shy but forceful Elie Wiesel at the Women's League Convention in 1966

With a far more self-assured Elie Wiesel some thirty years later

In the years after Al Fried died, teaching at Manhattan and then
Kingsborough Community College became my solace.
Here I am working with a group of students on a radio broadcast

Usher and I at our wedding with Arthur, Rabbi
Finkelstein (who officiated) and Alissa

At their home in Flatbush, Brooklyn — top:
Arthur, Alissa, Susan holding Debra; middle:
Abigail, Sara, Avi; bottom: Zipporah

Years later, shortly after I got married, I prepared my first dinner for some friends. For dessert, I made a lemon meringue pie using the recipe in the Ida Bailey Allen cookbook someone had given me as a wedding present. Everyone used that cookbook then. The pie rose very nicely. It looked great, and I was thrilled. But when I took it to the table and cut into it, the whole thing ran like water. The meringue didn't hold.

The next day Aunt Hannah called to find out how the dinner went. I said, "Oh, it was so good, except for the lemon meringue pie." And I told her what happened.

"No wonder," she said. "That's because you didn't want to use my recipe."

I think I became the closest person in the world to Aunt Hannah. And I felt so special that I was chosen to be her confidante. Only I knew that she could neither write nor read English, although she was able to sign her name with a real flourish. I did all her writing for her.

Aunt Hannah had a tremendous influence on me. Beyond being a model of sophistication and elegance, she was also very kind. The copper kettle from India that sits on my china closet to this day was a gift from her. She gave me many other gifts as well. But she never told me why she left Poland or what her life in India was really like beyond the generalities. In retrospect, I think she was not comfortable being in a world that was entirely gentile.

When she died, Aunt Hannah was buried in the family plot in Port Chester and eulogized by the same Rabbi Ginsburg who years before had chased me out of Hebrew school. He kept repeating what a true Jewish woman she was, so devout, so pious. I felt sick. Not one of those things was true. They were all platitudes. There were so many wonderful things one could say about Hannah. She was a beautiful and generous person. She had led such an interesting life. She had accomplished things few women of her generation hoped to accomplish. Why, I wondered, did he keep referring to the fact that she was kosher – which she was not – instead of trying to evoke what she was really like?

Then and there I decided that if I ever go to a funeral where the rabbi doesn't know the person who has died, I will make it my business to get to him before the funeral and tell him what I know about the deceased. And that is something I have done throughout my life.

One day my rich Aunt Annie came over to the house while I was practicing the piano. "You know, Helen darling, only with you would my Bernie take lessons," she said, speaking through her nose as she always did.

I didn't like Bernie or his brothers very much, but I couldn't refuse. So I began teaching Bernie how to play the piano. Then his brothers wanted to learn, and before you knew it, they had recommended me to others. Here I was, a high school girl, and I found myself traveling as far as the Bronx and charging fifty cents a lesson. It was terrific. I felt so important. Now I had more money to squirrel away along with the nickels I had pocketed a few years ago when I roller skated to my piano lessons instead of taking the trolley.

I found that I enjoyed teaching, that I got a kick out of imparting whatever knowledge I had. And so around that time, I asked my grandfather if I could teach a class in the B'nai Israel Sunday School. I had been watching one of the teachers, and it seemed to me she was too firm with the children and wasn't reaching them. "I can do that and better," I said to my grandfather. He thought I was the smartest little thing in the world, and before I knew it, he had arranged for me to teach a group of the younger children.

It was my first time before a class. The children were maybe six or seven years old, and we studied the bible stories that I had learned from the time I was very little. No one told me how to teach; I just kept one chapter ahead of the kids. And again I loved it. I felt like I was on stage.

Teaching Sunday School was volunteer work, but I also prevailed upon my grandfather to get me a real job where I would be paid. He set me up at Jonas Millinery in Bay Ridge, a shop that was a big, thriving business back when women did not consider themselves well dressed without a hat and pair of gloves.

After finishing a day of classes at New Utrecht High School, I would take the subway to Bay Ridge and put in my hours at Jonas Millinery. My specialty was the "P.M." or postmortem, which referred to a hat that had been lying around since the year before or earlier. If someone sold a postmortem, they earned another fifty cents. The experienced salespeople didn't want to be annoyed with the P.M.s, so they became my baby. If a woman walked in who didn't look very sophisticated, the others would say, "Let the kid take that one." I would take the hat, re-trim it with a feather or flower, and make the sale.

It was no problem to do the re-trimming because I had a great sense of color, and I loved to sew. Although Papa often brought me knitted outfits from the factory, I was a little chunky as a teenager and knitwear never seemed right for me. I much preferred making my own clothes.

In junior high school we had to sew our own graduation dresses. Many girls sneaked theirs home to have their mothers and grandmothers help them. But I made mine all by myself – even though it had a very complex panel shirred into the skirt.

By the time I was a student at New Utrecht High, I was making a lot of my own clothes using fine materials, often silk. I don't know where I got the guts to buy such expensive fabrics. If the dress came out badly, it would be terrible. Sometimes I used complicated patterns, but often as not, I'd make just a simple sheath with piping around the neck and sleeves in a contrasting color. For example, I'd make a dress of brown silk and trim it with pale orange.

Aviation was still pretty new then, and everyone was so excited about flying. My friends and I would go to Floyd Bennett Field on Flatbush Avenue to watch the airplanes take off and land. Once, a few of us took a short ride in an airplane. It was small and very open, and as it took off, I was scared to death. What am I doing, I thought. Then we flew up over the Rockaways and Jamaica Bay and saw all the way out to the ocean. It was so exhilarating.

After that, I began including aviation themes in my sewing. I would make an aviator's hat, cutting through the sides and inserting felt in the shape of wings in a contrasting color. Then I'd make a dress with a matching cape lined in the same contrasting color.

As I moved through my teens, I realized that although I was not beautiful, people would turn to look at me. At an early age, I had learned how to make the best out of what I had. Then again, perhaps my clothing had something to do with it.

III

GREEN INK

For my senior year of high school, I decided to transfer to Textile High in Manhattan. New Utrecht High had no courses in dress-design and pattern-making, and I was becoming more and more interested in becoming a dress designer.

Leaving New Utrecht High School meant I would have to leave my whole social world in Brooklyn and schlep by subway from Bensonhurst to Manhattan every day. How my mother ever agreed to let me go, I can't imagine. But being one never to waste time, I took along tablecloths to embroider on those long train rides.

Everybody had heard about Textile High in those days. It was a coed school with a mixed student body, located in the Garment District, where the Fashion Institute of Technology is today. I took some wonderful courses there. And though I never went into dress designing professionally, I felt my senior year was very well spent at Textile High, especially since I went on to design and sew so many of my clothes.

At first I didn't know anybody there. Then I met Lenore, a black girl who lived uptown, probably in Harlem. She became my dearest friend. Lenore never walked, she danced, which was not surprising as she wanted to be a dancer and took dancing classes in gym.

Each Wednesday afternoon, together with Lenore, some other school friends, or all by myself, I would go to see a Broadway show. Most of the theaters were just half a mile uptown and tickets cost less than fifty-five cents. I saw Sigmund Romberg operettas and the Ziegfeld Follies; I saw Al

Jolson and Eddie Cantor. At one point, they called my mother from school to find out why I was absent so often on Wednesdays. She was beside herself. "They call me from the school, and I don't know where you are." But I loved the theater and couldn't resist the lure of the Wednesday matinee.

That June I graduated from Textile High School. I had an academic diploma; still, I decided not to go on to college. My parents were furious. I was always a good student. My father was doing well by that time, so I didn't have to go to work. My grandfather was terribly disappointed. He was certain I was going to become a lawyer – although I don't know how he got that idea – and gave me a tome of Jewish jurisprudence as a graduation present. "Money goes through your hands," he used to say. "You'll get money later on. Now you have to go to school."

But I wouldn't listen. I wanted to earn money. I wanted to buy the high-heeled shoes Mama refused to get me and the clothes I wanted to wear. After all, I couldn't sew my entire wardrobe.

I had heard there was a school in the Wall Street area called the Elliot Fischer Electric Bookkeeping Machine School, where they trained you to operate this new electric bookkeeping machine. I decided to go there. My parents, angry over my not going to college, refused to pay for the course. But I had the money that I'd squirreled away and paid for it myself.

Ever since I was accepted in the Port Chester kindergarten, I have always sat up front in the very first row. And that's where I was when a gentleman came into the classroom one day. Being up front, I was able to overhear his conversation with the teacher.

"I must have somebody," he said.

"I don't have anyone who is finished yet," she told him. "The girls still have to pick up their speed."

He looked around. "There must be someone whom you can suggest who is more advanced than the others."

Impulsively, I raised my hand. "I think I can do the job," I called out. "I know the machine very, very well. I'll pick up speed on the job."

The man looked at me, turned to my teacher, and said, "I'll take a chance on that kid."

Looking back, I guess the other girls must have hated me. But I didn't feel their hate then. I didn't really. Anyhow I ignored them. I was just so anxious to finish the course and get a job.

The man explained the job was at Manufacturers' Trust Company, and it would only last for a few months. A big stock transfer had to be completed, and they were short on staff. That was fine with me. I'd have the chance to pick up my speed while making what seemed like a wonderful salary.

When the Manufacturers' Trust job ended, I found out there was an opening for an electric bookkeeper at the Auto Truck Garage on East Twenty-third Street and Avenue A. A distinguished looking elderly gentleman, who spoke with a Southern accent, interviewed me from behind an enormous rolltop desk. He was eating an apple that suddenly got stuck in his teeth. Nonchalantly, he pulled out his dentures, and while I pretended not to see, removed the apple, put the teeth back in his mouth, and continued the interview.

Whatever he asked of me, I said I could do it.

"Can you take stenography?"

Well, of course I couldn't. But I noticed he spoke very slowly and deliberately, so I said, "I can't take shorthand as you know it. But I can write very quickly. I can handle it."

"Can you keep a set of books?"

"Oh, yes."

I didn't know any bookkeeping back then. But Sam Goodman, a young man I was dating at the time, had told me, "Tell him you can do elementary bookkeeping, and I'll show you what to do."

I was hired, and I stayed at Auto Truck Garage for quite a few years, moving up to the position of chief bookkeeper. Sam, true to his word, trained me. He used to wait outside the office, and when the chauffeur came to pick up the boss, he'd come in and teach me how to keep a set of books. By the time I left that job, I was an A-number-one bookkeeper.

I also was an A-number-one gas-pumper. The huge trucks stored in the garage had to be filled with gas before they went out in the morning. I always used to go into the garage to kibitz around with the guys and would always end up pumping gas.

Sam Goodman was a student at New York University then. "Helen, you must go to college," he kept telling me. But that was just more of what I heard at home, so I remained unconvinced until he prevailed upon me to sit in on the commercial law class he was taking. "The professor is from the family of President Cleveland," he said, thinking that would be an attraction. I gave in and agreed to let Sam schlep me along.

Well, after that one session, I was hooked on higher education. In fact, I found the commercial law class so fascinating, I decided I would go to college after all and then go on to law school.

At the start of the next semester, I went down to NYU to register for the same course Sam had taken. The registrar said to me, "You know if you register for only this three-credit course, you won't get any credit."

I said, "I don't want any credit."

He said, "But if you matriculate…"

I heard that word "matriculate." I had no idea what it meant, but it sounded like something very sexy. I let him continue.

"If you take two courses, you'll get six credits," he explained. "That will put you on a line of matriculation that will lead to a college degree."

It seemed like a good deal, and I was always one to look for a bargain. So I registered for a second course at the rate of eight dollars a credit. And that was the beginning of my college career.

The commercial law class was taught by Professor Cleveland Bacon, a short, robust man and a memorable character. Professor Bacon wasn't dressed together; he was thrown together. Nothing ever matched. He would attach his socks with a safety pin to his long underwear, and it was rare that his two socks matched.

Most of the students who took night courses had worked all day. They were tired and often they would doze off during class. But you couldn't doze off in Bacon's class because in the midst of some theoretical point, he would insert a correct and appropriate little story that would awaken anyone. Come to think of it, just looking at him would keep you awake.

I quickly found I had a coterie of friends at NYU. Most of them were boys, because few women went to college back then, especially at night. We would ride the subways together, and as I was always embroidering, I taught them how to cross-stitch. They'd do the napkins, I'd do the tablecloth, and in a few weeks we'd complete a set.

The practice at NYU during those years was to send the name of any student who made Dean's List to the principal of the high school from which he or she had graduated. At the end of my first semester, I made Dean's List, and Dr. Dooley, the principal of Textile High, was notified. He got in touch with me and invited me to come and see him.

"What are your plans when you finish college?" he asked me.

"Well, I don't know," I replied. "I was thinking of law."

"No," he said. "Consider teaching. You'll make a wonderful teacher. And when you are qualified to teach, come back to me, and I will see that you get a job right here at Textile High."

Well, I thought, this is sensational. How great it'll be to go back to Textile High as a teacher. I kept his promise in mind, and as soon as I graduated, I got in touch with Dr. Dooley. But he didn't remember me at all.

What a disappointment! I was crushed. Nevertheless, Dr. Dooley had done me a service. His suggestion stuck in my mind. I knew that I wanted to become a teacher, and it wouldn't matter what subject I would teach. I had already taught Sunday School and piano. In years to come, I'd teach bookkeeping and typing, speech and theater, and even mah-jongg.

For now, though, I continued working at the Auto Truck Garage and going to NYU at night. Although I was enrolled in the evening school, six-year baccalaureate program, I took courses over the summer and often registered for classes that began at 4:00 in the afternoon. In this way, I was able to complete the six-year evening program in four years, becoming the first girl at NYU to accomplish that feat.

For most of this time, I continued seeing Sam Goodman. Sam was very good to me. He took me out nicely. We went to all the NYU basketball games and other functions. He was good looking as well, and he came from a fine family. His father was a kosher butcher, and kosher butchers in those days did very nicely. More importantly, his butcher shop was in Brooklyn Heights, and as a result of buying property in the neighborhood, he became very wealthy. But I could never relate to Sam the way he wanted to relate to me. He was short, and I have never been attracted to short men.

Sam's cousin, Aaron, obviously disliked me. I couldn't understand it at the time. It was only later on that I realized Aaron could tell I wasn't in love with his cousin and was using him to have someone to go out with.

In the summers, my mother would rent an apartment in Coney Island or Sea Gate. One day Sam, Aaron, and I were walking down Stillwell Avenue in Coney Island when we passed one of those penny arcades with a big scale out front.

"I don't know what my cousin sees in you," Aaron suddenly said to me. "You're so fat. I bet you weigh 150 pounds."

"I do not," I said indignantly.

He put a penny in the scale and said, "Get on it."

It was a dare. I knew I wasn't anywhere near 150 pounds so I got on the scale, but as the needle passed 135, I jumped off. I didn't want to know how much I weighed.

At that moment, I decided I was going to lose weight. I was 5' 1" and pudgy, but I was determined to get thinner.

I went on a crazy prune diet. There was a two-burner in the back of the office at Auto Truck Garage where I boiled prunes in a little pot. I had stewed prunes for lunch every day. Sometimes I had stewed prunes for dinner too. And little by little, about fifteen pounds came off. At that point, I treated myself to a beautiful suit at Fisher Brothers on Division Street.

All the while I kept dating Sam, never exclusively, but he didn't know that – at least I never told him. There were others, like Ray Rivoli, whose father was the president of the Italian-American Bank. Unlike Sam, Ray was tall. He was also very handsome. Any girl would have flipped if she were asked out by him.

For our second date, we were going to a costume ball. Ray sent me to a theatrical costume company where I got this beautiful turn-of-the-last century ensemble: a long organza lavender dress with ruffles down the front and on the sleeves, and a flowered hat and parasol to match. Ray waited outside my house for me – I could never ask a non-Jewish boy to come into the house – and I could tell from his expression he thought I looked great.

It was a wonderful evening. By the time we came home, it was rather late. Whenever I went out, Mama went to sleep at her usual time, but Papa waited up until he heard me. Then he'd open up the window and call down in Yiddish, "Helen, is that you? Goodnight darling."

Somehow with Ray, I felt terribly embarrassed and ashamed hearing my father speaking in Yiddish. I also felt terribly resentful that he was checking up on me. But my overwhelming emotion was guilt. I knew I was betraying my father by going out with someone who wasn't Jewish. And I decided there and then I would never see Ray again.

The last year I went to NYU, I shared a one-room-plus-kitchen apartment on Minetta Lane in Greenwich Village with a school chum. I persuaded my parents that I had to have an apartment. After all, I didn't get out of school until 8:00 at night. I had to take the train and then the bus to get home. I worked, I went to school, I dated. I did lots of things. It was too much.

My apartment mate was Anne Himmelstein, a girl from a well-to-do family in Hartford, Connecticut. Often she'd come home with me for the weekends. But we loved living in the Village. We had a phonograph and played popular music day and night. We'd look out the window and find people out on the streets all the time. Something was always happening.

One night it was so hot I couldn't sleep. I was wearing a thin nightgown, but even that was uncomfortable. So I took it off and tossed it across the room expecting it would land on a chair. Somehow it sailed out the open window instead. I had to get dressed and go downstairs to retrieve my nightgown under some very curious stares. But that was fun; it was something you'd expect to happen living in Greenwich Village.

Once I began dating the man I married, Anne moved away from our friendship. Whether she was doing it for my sake or because she was jealous, I never knew. If I invited her to join us, she declined. She was no longer comfortable sleeping over at our house on weekends. We drifted apart and ultimately gave up the apartment.

But by then, my life had taken a different and very happy turn that began one evening when a friend of mine came into the ladies' room at NYU with a stack of Season's Greetings cards that her boss at A&S had given her.

"I don't know what to do with these, Helen," she said to me. "Would you like some? I have so many, and I don't know whom to send them to."

I said, "I've got an idea. Let's send them to the guys we'd like to meet. We can sign our name on the bottom, put our return address on the back of the envelope, and see what happens."

"What a great idea!" she said, and that's what we did.

In those days, I always used green ink. It was very unusual at the time; I thought of it as my trademark. Now I selected one of the cards and in green ink I signed it "Helen Feiner." I put my return address on the back of the envelope, and mailed the card to Al Fried.

When I first laid eyes on Al Fried, he was a student at New Utrecht High School in Brooklyn and two years ahead of me. He was absolutely drop-dead handsome. In fact he was voted the best-looking boy in his graduating class. He was also into all kinds of sports and an excellent golfer, which was unique for a Brooklyn boy in those days.

His younger sister, Ethel, was in some of my classes, and I befriended her hoping that I'd get to meet him that way. But my plan didn't work. And as for Al Fried, he never noticed me. He wouldn't look at the chubby little kid I was back then.

But somehow I kept him in my heart all these years. And when I decided I was going to lose weight, I also decided that somehow I would get in touch with him. Now I had lost the weight and had become attractive, and when this girl came in with the cards, I saw my opportunity.

The following Sunday afternoon, I was alone in the house studying for an exam when the phone rang. It was Al Fried. "I got a card from you," he said, not having any idea who I was.

"A card?" I denied sending it. I was so scared that I didn't even want to talk to him.

But we got into a conversation. Even then I was a good conversationalist. He ended up saying, "You know, you sound very nice. I'd like to meet you. Can I come over to your house?"

"Well, I don't think so," I said, not wanting to appear overanxious. "I'm very busy. I'm studying for an exam tomorrow. And I have to get up early to go to work." Evidently, he liked what he heard. Because by telling him he couldn't come over, I was telling him a lot about myself.

Then I realized he wasn't pushing all that hard, and I wondered whether I was handling it well. After all, this was the chance I had been waiting for. So I said, "All right, but you have to take two buses to get here."

He lived in Bensonhurst, and we were living in Marine Park by this time. "I know how to get there," he said.

I can tell you today what I wore. My father had brought home a knitted top for me that was very becoming. It was one of the few knitted garments I liked, with green and black horizontal stripes, a square neckline, and short sleeves. I wore it with a trim black skirt. At the last minute, I put on a string of pearls.

The moment I opened the door and saw Al Fried standing there is indelibly marked on my life. I asked him in. We sat in the living room and talked. Then my parents came home, surprised to see I had a guest. They thought I was home alone studying all day. My mother called me into the kitchen. "Who's the shmegeggie in there with the white socks?" she asked.

"Oh, he's someone from school."

Al and I started dating right away, and I stopped seeing everyone else. The following summer he worked as a caddy for a hotel in the White Mountains of New Hampshire, and I did not date anyone all that time. He never called because that was too expensive, but he sent me love letters written on the bark of white birch trees – he had that romantic strain.

I did feel guilty about dropping Sam. We never had a discussion. I just stopped accepting dates with him. He'd call and I'd say, "I can't see you because…" and I'd make up some excuse. Finally he learned through the grapevine that I was dating somebody else. He was heartbroken.

Friends of his would call me up and ask, "How could you do this to Sam?" Not his cousin Aaron of course. Aaron wouldn't have anything to do with me.

It was very difficult. Sam was so good to me and to my family as well. When my parents were shopping for a house in Marine Park, a new neighborhood in Brooklyn, he was their real estate specialist. He helped them with the contract. He encouraged them to buy the only detached house on a block of semi-attached houses. "It's a little more money but you'll be much happier here and you're probably not going to miss the money," Sam said. They listened to him, and he was correct.

Years later, when I learned that Sam was happily married with several daughters, I was very glad because I felt I had loused him up terribly. I was the mother of two sons by then and realized how terrible I would feel if one of my boys were treated the way I treated Sam. He was an A-number-one guy and such a positive influence in my life. I wish I knew where he is now, because I'd like to apologize.

As for Al Fried, it wasn't until after we were married that I told him how I had had such a crush on him back in New Utrecht High School. My other secret was revealed much earlier. Soon after we began seeing each other, he happened to pick up one of my school notebooks and saw the writing in green ink. We both laughed then, and I confessed to my deed. After Al died, I found the Season's Greetings card I'd sent him among his papers. He had saved it all those years.

PART TWO

IV

A YOUNG WIFE AND MOTHER

Mama and papa said to me, "Helen, we can make a real nice wedding for you, or we can give you the money." I hesitated for a moment. Al Fried looked at me, but he said nothing. It was up to me to make the decision.

As much as I always appreciated money, I said, "I want a wedding."

We were married on June 30, 1935 at the Masonic Temple in Bensonhurst. It was a beautiful wedding, I must tell you. It really was.

I designed my own wedding gown with the help of Millicent, Hy's fiancée. Nettie and I had done whatever we could to discourage Hy from marrying his previous girlfriend who was much taller than him and, I thought, made him look less important. But we approved of Millicent from day one. She came from a fine family in the Bronx. Both her brothers were doctors. And Millicent was very artistic; she drew the figure of my wedding gown on white paper.

I knew just what I wanted the gown to look like. The material had to be Alencon lace; that is the kind of lace where heavy embroidery is superimposed on a net background, creating an intricate pattern. The gown had to have a bullet sleeve, which is like a series of rounded pleats that add height to the shoulders, and end with a tight, pointed edge just beyond the wrist. It had to have the bullets on the top of the train, which would then flange out, a tiny Peter Pan collar, a tight waist, and a skirt full enough to walk nicely. It came out just as I had envisioned it.

I made my future mother-in-law's dress as well, although for hers I used a pattern. She was a big woman, tall and angular, very handsome. It was absolutely correct for her.

During the wedding, I was in a cubicle in the ladies' room when some women came in. I recognized their voices. They were my three cousins from Port Chester, Fannie and two Helens. I actually had three cousins in Port Chester named Helen. All of us were named after the same grandmother. It got so confusing that for a while, I insisted my name was Joy just to distinguish myself from the other three Helens.

Now I heard one of the Helens say, "Oh, doesn't Helen look beautiful?" And the other Helen said, "Oh yes, and her dress is so lovely." But Fannie said, "Humph! All brides are beautiful."

Well, I thought, that isn't true. I've seen some pretty ugly brides. And from that moment on, I disliked Fannie.

But I began to look at myself more closely. And when we got the wedding pictures back, I saw there was a little bump on my nose. Somehow I had never noticed it before. Now it began to bother me.

A few months after Al and I were married, Nettie married Sam Feldman, a salesman with a terrific outgoing personality. A few months after that, Hy married Millicent. In the space of one year, all my mother's children got married, and none of us changed our monograms.

Nettie didn't want a wedding, so my mother gave her money and she bought a car. But with Nettie and Hy getting married and moving out of the house, my parents urged Al Fried and me to live with them. The idea seemed like a good one. It was common at that time for generations to live together, as many young couples couldn't afford to rent their own apartment during the Depression. We would contribute a minimal amount. My parents didn't need the money, and we were building up our savings. So we agreed. And as it turned out, the house in Marine Park was to be Al Fried's and my home for all the years of our life together.

Mama and Papa had bought the house in 1933 brand new. It had two stories, three bedrooms upstairs, a large living room, a dining room, and kitchen downstairs, and a big basement. But it was the upstairs bathroom that really sold the house. The tiles were peach. It had a stall shower, which was unheard of in those days, a toilet to match the tiles, a gorgeous colored bathtub that I luxuriated in, and even a dressing table.

When they first moved in, Mama and Papa took the back bedroom because it was quieter, being off the street. Nettie and I shared the front bedroom, and Hy had the smaller bedroom in the hall. Now Al and I had the bedroom I had previously shared with Nettie.

But I wanted to furnish it to suit my own tastes. Al and I went to this big furniture store on Kings Highway and bought a bedroom set in off-white wood. It had a double bed, a triple dresser with a mirror, a tall chest of drawers, and two night tables with lamps. We carpeted the floor with turquoise wall-to-wall broadloom. This room was the first place in the house that I established my identity as a married woman.

As a young girl, I never was told anything about sex. I felt my mother didn't enjoy it, and that always bothered me. There were times I thought maybe I shouldn't either. Whatever I knew I picked up from girlfriends or magazines, and there wasn't much discussion of sex in magazines back then. I noticed though that whenever a boy would get near me and press his body against mine, his penis was very hard. I thought that was the way it stayed all the time. "You've got a lot to learn, darling," Al said when I shared my impression with him.

It was Eva Ezra, who became one of my two best friends in Marine Park, who enlightened me about sex. She was very open about it. "Whatever your husband wants you to do, you do it," Eva would tell me. "Even if you think it's not right or that you won't like it, do it anyway." At first that didn't sit well with me. But I learned that she was right, and that is one of the things that makes for a good marriage.

After we got married, I continued working at Auto Truck Garage, and Al Fried continued his accountant's apprenticeship with Max Posner, the husband of his sister, Ida. That was the way accountants began in those days. Max only paid him eight dollars a week, which I thought was ridiculously low. I was making twenty-five dollars a week at Auto Truck Garage.

As long as he was single, Al Fried gave his mother the money he earned. His father was a tailor, and they often needed something extra to make ends meet. I didn't mind. I really didn't. Money didn't mean that much to me. And then, after we got married, my mother-in-law presented us with a bankbook. It turned out she had deposited the eight dollars every week into a joint account that she had set up for herself and Al.

I loved Al's mother. We were very close. My mother was also fond of her. But as a young bride, I didn't realize there's always a little competition between a mother and mother-in-law, and that it wasn't so wise to tell my mother everything my mother-in-law told me. Al's mother was a terrific cook, and at one time she told me that the secret to making a delicious chicken soup is to add a pinch of sugar to the pot. I shared this suggestion with my mother. "That's ridiculous. I never heard of such a thing," she said huffily.

Then, one Friday morning, when I was making chicken soup and Nettie and Mama were sitting in the living room, I overheard Mama tell Nettie, "I'll give you a tip. But don't tell anyone; keep it in the family. When you're cooking a chicken, add a drop or two of sugar to the soup so the chicken will taste sweet."

The first year we were married, Al and I bought a four-door, green Dodge. I insisted on four doors because I didn't like the idea of having to open the door and slide over to let people squeeze in. It wouldn't be comfortable for them, and it wouldn't be comfortable for me.

We used the Dodge for our belated honeymoon, a motor trip to upper New York State and into Canada as far as Quebec. When my friend Mildred Solomon heard about it, she said she had to come along. Mildred was the daughter of Charles Solomon, a well-known judge who ran for governor on the Socialist ticket. We'd been friends since high school. She was quite theatrical and was the first person I knew who went to Paris. She came back with a gift for me, a lipstick. Was I thrilled – a lipstick from Paris! I used it sparingly so it would last a long time. But one day, I happened to turn it over, and guess what it said? "Made in Brooklyn."

I was pushing for Mildred to get married. Her boyfriend, Vincent DePaul Clinton, was a terrific guy, and they had been going together a long time. Clinton was Catholic. He came from a very observant family; his sisters were nuns. But he was not religious, and at that time I didn't think so much about intermarriage.

I said to her, "I don't think it would be very nice if you came along with us if you and Clinton weren't married." In order to go on this trip with us, they decided to get married, and they went down to City Hall.

Although they decided not to have children, they had a wonderful marriage that ended when Clinton died of cancer at a very young age. It was the first time someone I knew well had that disease. We never called it cancer, just "the c-thing." We couldn't say the word.

But Mildred went on to have a very successful acting career in film, theater, and television. One of her best-known roles was the mother in the movie *Serpico*. She's remained a close family friend.

That summer when we were newlyweds, we stayed in lovely old homes with bedrooms reserved for guests, what today you would call "bed and breakfasts." Usually these places would have one bedroom that was much nicer than the other. We'd switch off. One night Mildred and Clinton would get the better room, and the next night Al and I would take it.

On the way back in Cohoes, New York, it was our turn to get the better room. We walked into a big, beautiful bedroom, and there hanging over the bed was an enormous crucifix with a very realistic depiction of Jesus. Al and I looked at each other. How could we sleep with a cross over our heads? We ran to take a look at the smaller and much more modest second bedroom. No crucifix. Mildred and Clinton lucked out. They had the bigger, better bedroom two nights in a row.

While Al was a student at St. John's University, he had become very friendly with the guys on the championship basketball team. After graduation, they turned professional and went around playing other teams. We traveled all over with them. Max Posnack, one of the teammates, had a girlfriend who looked just like Jean Harlow, very sensual with platinum hair and big breasts, although the rest of her was quite thin. I made a lot of mileage on her breasts. The boys were attracted to her for that and to me for other things. We were a good team that way.

Al and I would fill up the car with some of the guys and go up to the Catskills, where the "Wonder Five Team," as they were called, played against other basketball teams in places like the Concord or Grossinger's. Generally it was during the time of changing seasons. The roads were terrible, and the weather wasn't too good. But that didn't matter to us. We never stayed over. Who would spend the money on a hotel? We just went for the games.

During these first few years of our marriage, I couldn't get over the fact that I had been able to garner one of the top prizes among the young Jewish boys of that time – although, of course, I didn't let Al know I felt that way. He was so desirable, absolutely gorgeous, with large blue-green eyes and a physique that stood up nice and straight. At New Utrecht High School he had been a golf champion and won medals for swimming and diving. He was very clean about himself and well mannered. Not a bag of wind, he was someone who made sense when he spoke, whom people respected.

To his family, Al Fried was an idol. He was the youngest boy and the only one to graduate from college. He was also very considerate of his elders, always treating my parents with respect. Can you imagine the four of us living together, later on with the children, and I don't recall a time when any of us raised our voices in anger.

Al Fried was everything a woman could want, not pushy but gentlemanly-like. I was very much in love with him and so proud that I had hooked him. I had tried very hard, and I had made it happen with him.

Early on in our marriage, we went to the Nevele Hotel in the Catskills for a week. A very attractive woman from the Prospect Park Jewish Center was seated next to him at our table in the dining room. I can see her in front of me to this very day. Her husband only came up on weekends, and during that week, she really made a play for Al. It was very obvious. She moved so close to him, she was practically sitting on his chair. And the way she spoke to him was definitely not the way she spoke to me.

It really bothered me, and at first I didn't know how to handle it. After a few days, however, I understood I would have to take the situation in hand. I said something to Al, we changed our table, and that was the end of it. There were many women who eyed Al. I knew it; I saw it. But until then, I had never met anyone like this woman – a married woman – who would make such an obvious play for someone else's husband right in front of his wife.

Once, my mother, Nettie, and I were sitting around the kitchen table and somehow we got to talking about infidelity. My mother said, "I would trust Papa, I would trust Sammy, I would trust Hy, and I would trust Al. No woman could get to them."

"Mama," I said, "I wouldn't trust Papa, Sammy, Hy, or Al. You never know who could get to a man."

A man's head can be turned. I believe that, I really do.

Before long, Al took the examination to be a Certified Public Accountant. He passed the first time round, left Max Posner, and got a job with Ernst and Ernst, a very fine public accounting firm. Meanwhile I decided to go back to NYU for a master's degree in secondary education. I again took my courses at night until it was time for me to do my student-teaching. Then I finally had to leave Auto Truck Garage, the place that had served me so well for so many years.

In the fall term, I student-taught at a school in Newark, New Jersey. But the traveling was very difficult, and I was happy to be able to land a slot at the Rhodes School for the spring semester, along with my friend Rivia Mishnoff, who also happened to be the daughter of my dentist.

Rhodes School was a private school on Sixth Avenue, across the street from the main branch of the New York Public Library. Most of the students were spoiled brats who came from well-to-do homes and were often difficult to control. I taught commercial law, which I liked, and bookkeeping, which I liked less.

Before my term was over, the principal, Dr. Goodman, offered me a regular job beginning the next fall. This was 1938, during the Depression, when it was a big deal to get a teaching job. Rivia was not offered a job, and that affected our friendship for a while.

But it picked up again when Rivia began dating Harry Gasarch, one of the '34-ers, a group we both belonged to, named for the year we got our bachelor's degrees from NYU. Rivia and I were the only girls in this crowd. The guys were the ones whom I had taught to embroider on the subway rides into the city, years ago. Now we'd get together at each other's homes periodically. Harry Gasarch had a crush on me. But just as I knew instinctively that Al Fried was right for me, I knew Harry Gasarch was not. He was very bright though, and in those days, when Jewish boys had to change their names in order to get a good job, Harry was able to land a job at one of the big oil companies without changing his name. He became very successful and ended up marrying Rivia.

One day during my first semester of teaching at the Rhodes School, Dr. Goodman came into my room and asked me to stop by his office before I left for the day. He had something very serious to discuss with me. All afternoon I wondered, what did he want to see me about? Had I done something wrong?

Finally the school day ended and I entered his office. He began by telling me what a wonderful job I was doing. Then he said, "Helen, you must do me a big favor. Mrs. Schlessinger can't control her classes. The students are running all over the place. You've got to take over her typing classes."

"I can't do that," I told him. "I don't know how to type."

"You don't have to know how to type," he said. "You can teach anything."

The next semester began. Mrs. Schlessinger was fired, and I was the new typing teacher. For weeks before, I tried to find out how to teach typing, how to maintain interest, how to keep the kids absorbed. But nothing I read seemed to be what was needed.

Then I got an idea. Typing is rhythmic. Why not have the kids type to music? I got a portable phonograph, brought it to class along with some recordings of light classical music, and had the students type along to the rhythm of the songs. It worked.

But during that term, I started to have a recurring dream. I am in the typing room about to give a test. "All right," I say to the kids. "Put your papers in the machine and be prepared to type sixty words a minute."

Suddenly I see Dr. Goodman is watching me through the window of the classroom door. He enters the room. "I'd like to see you type sixty words a minute," he whispers to me.

I become very flustered. I don't know what to do. "My typewriter is in the back of the room," I tell him. "Let's go back there. I can do more than sixty words a minute. I'll show you."

We walk to the back of the room. I sit down before the typewriter, and, looking very professional, I put my hands on the keys and begin to type. Dr. Goodman tries to come around to see what I am typing. Of course, it is gibberish. So what I do is continue typing with my right hand while with my left hand, I keep pushing him back so he can't see what I'm doing. He keeps approaching, and I keep pushing.

For some reason, that dream haunted me. I've had it over and over for years and years.

I never did learn to type, and I never did enjoy the teaching of typing. But I loved working in the Rhodes School's theater program. We did a comedy called *Growing Pains*. The entire production was my responsibility; I had to get the rights to the play, cast it, stage it, direct it, and produce it.

There was an auditorium in the Rhodes School but it was very small, so one of the first things I had to do was to find a theater. Somehow I learned that the theater around the corner, on West Forty-first Street was the Mercury Theater, associated with Orson Welles. I managed to get a face-to-face meeting with him, and he not only agreed to let us use his theater at no charge, he seemed happy to do so, pleased that this school around the corner had a theatrical program.

One day while we were rehearsing, Orson Welles came in. He sat in the back, and afterwards he came down to the front. He said many encouraging things to us and wished us well.

Our play went exceedingly well. Producing *Growing Pains* was the highlight of my time at the Rhodes School. And theater wasn't even my field. I wasn't prepared academically to direct a play. But therein lay the challenge – to do something I was not quite qualified to do.

Because of the Depression, Al Fried and I waited six years until we had children. But during that time, we had the pleasure of babies without the responsibilities. My half-sister, Chaneleh, would visit my parents often with her husband, Joe Kleiner, and their little boy, Howard. Sandy and Allan, Ida and Max's boys, were like our own children, spending weekends with us. We took them to ball games and the circus. Sandy, in particular, was very attached to me. He loved to come over to our house and hang around in my bedroom while I was sewing or doing some paperwork.

During my third year of teaching at the Rhodes School, I discovered I was pregnant. At that time, you couldn't continue to teach if you were expecting. So I made these unusual smocks – one I remember in particular was a gorgeous chintz print of the world – and ended up with a fantastic wardrobe that covered up my condition.

We female teachers had to check the girls' room periodically. One day, I opened the door and a girl who had been in my class was there. "Oh, Mrs. Fried," she said when she noticed me, "can I see your hand?"

"Why?" I asked.

"Oh, please."

I showed her my hand. She looked at it very seriously and said, "You're going to have a baby girl."

I stuttered and stumbled. "What makes you think I'm pregnant?" I asked.

"Oh, all the kids know it."

Immediately, I walked into Dr. Goodman's office and told him the story. "Please don't tell anybody else," he said. "I want you to work out the term."

I worked until the end of June and gave birth the end of July.

Back when I was a little girl in Port Chester, we used to play on the big porch in front of Tante Chana Blima's house. One day, a bunch of us were running up and down the steps and making a lot of noise when a grown-up came out and shouted, "Shhh, children! Be quiet! Don't you know, Chana Blima is giving birth!"

We quieted down only to hear Tante Chana Blima's screams from inside the house.

I looked at my cousins. "I'm never going to have a baby," I declared.

But I did have two wonderful babies who grew into two splendid men. My pregnancies were wonderful, and, unlike Tante Chana Blima, I had easy deliveries.

Arthur was born with red hair. I have always said that he made an honest woman out of me, although to tell the truth, I had been helping nature along from the time I was a teenager and ran a comb dipped in peroxide through my hair. I remember when my grandfather told me, "Helen, your hair is so shining and beautiful just like you," and I felt a little guilty about my peroxide secret. Still, I kept it up. Later on, I used the Clairol dye, mixing the colors to get just the shade I wanted. And that was exactly the shade of hair Arthur was born with.

In those days you stayed in the hospital for a week. It was great. People came to see you and brought you flowers and gifts. Arthur was the first baby in our family, and everyone was so happy over his arrival.

But after a few days, the doctor came in and told me, "Helen, you're going home." I wasn't ready to go home. I was having a wonderful time. But he insisted. Later I discovered that there was a terrible epidemic in the nursery of the Madison Hospital on Kings Highway. A few babies had died. As a result, they cleaned out the nursery and sent all the mothers and infants home.

I had arranged for a baby nurse for the first week. But as soon as I met Pauline, I realized she was taking charge. She wasn't going to let me do anything. Before the week was over, I nearly pushed her out of the door. Then I walked over to the crib, picked up the baby, and he vomited right in my face. Boy, I said to myself, here I was looking forward to twin girls and I can't even take care of one baby.

I pulled myself together, but it was difficult for me. Arthur was a colicky baby; he suffered from spells of indigestion because of the hospital infection, and it took a while before we got his formula adjusted so that he could hold it down.

There was no question whether I would go back to work after the baby was born. I loved teaching. I felt creative, productive, and proud to be a teacher at such a prestigious institution as the Rhodes School. But no sooner was I alone with Arthur, than I realized that he needed me. I suppose I could have relied on my mother to take care of the baby and gone back to teaching. But that wasn't what I wanted. I was determined to be home with my newborn child.

What I discovered is that your first baby is like no other baby in the world. Others will follow, and you will do your very best to be the perfect mother to the next child or children. Still, nothing can ever be the same as that first child.

When I became pregnant with Michael, I was sure it was going to be a girl, maybe even twin girls. I had visions of the mother-daughter outfits I was going to make for the three of us. The first time around, I had hoped for a girl. But when Arthur was born, I thought, okay, this baby is for Al, to carry on the name. The next one will be for me.

A week before I was due, I told Al, "Get me to the hospital."

"But you're not due yet."

"Al, get me to the hospital."

The nurse took a look at me. "You're not ready yet," she said.

"I am, I know I am," I told her.

Ten minutes later she came back to check on me. "Oh my God, you're ready," she said. "Hold the baby back!"

They put me on a gurney and wheeled me into the delivery room, crying, "Hold the baby back!"

The first thing I said was, "What is it?"

"Helen, I told you it was going to be a boy," Doctor Kane said. "And that's what it is, a nice healthy boy."

"A boy?" I screamed, I cried, I carried on like a lunatic, which was surprising because I was known as such a stable person. They wheeled me, sobbing, into a room with three other new mothers. One of them was an Italian woman who spoke with a heavy accent. "Whatsa the matter with her?" she asked the nurse. "She losta the baby?"

The nurse said, "Nah, she's crazy. She's crying because she didn't have a girl."

The woman turned to me. "Whatsa the matter with you? You crazy? I got five bambinos, all boys. Boys are better than girls."

She stopped me from crying, but I was inconsolable. Al Fried came to see me. "What do you want to call the baby?" he asked.

I had only prepared a girl's name: Rose Alice, Rose after my grandmother, Alice because I loved that name. "Call him anything you like," I said turning away.

"Well, we should use the letter J. How about Jeffrey?"

"I don't care."

Al registered the baby as Jeffrey Michael. Then, when I came to my senses and saw the birth announcements Al had printed, I said, "Oh, I don't like the name Jeffrey at all. It's very weak. I want a strong name for this boy. Let's use Michael."

So we called him J. Michael Fried. That's how he was registered in school, and with this name, Michael has gone through life.

For the first nine months, he was a healthy baby, thank God. Then he started to lose weight. We took him from one doctor to another, but no one could figure out what was wrong. It got worse and worse. We were desperate.

One day Millicent called me. "You have to bring Michael to Dr. Haus on East Eighty-sixth Street in Manhattan."

"I can't go to Manhattan," I said. "It's so far, and there are all these wonderful doctors here in Brooklyn."

"Helen, my nieces and nephews went through something like what Michael is going through. I would take him there if I were you."

The night before my appointment with Dr. Haus I said to Al Fried, "I know you can't come with me. But I've never driven over the Brooklyn Bridge before. I'm so frightened."

He said to me, "Helen, the bridge isn't any different from the street, except that it's all going one way and it's wider than a street. So when you are going over, say to yourself, 'This is a street. It's not a bridge.'"

I used that mantra. The baby was alongside me, all cuddled up in blankets, and I drove across the bridge saying, "This is a street. It's not a bridge. This is a street. It's not a bridge," over and over and over.

It turned out Dr. Haus was a specialist in celiac, a disorder where the digestive system cannot digest sugars and starches. And that was exactly what was wrong with this baby.

For the next two or three years, we had to keep Michael on a special diet. At first it was just milk and bananas. Al Fried used to go to the docks and get a whole big hand of bananas. We'd keep it in the basement, bringing up a few to ripen in the kitchen every week. And on this diet, very gradually, Michael became well again.

Around the time he was beginning to go back to normal food, we were driving home from the Catskills one afternoon and passed this place where we always stopped for ice cream. Michael had never been allowed to have it before. This time I said, "Michael, now you can have ice cream too. What flavor would you like?"

Our car was a green Plymouth then, which may have inspired his response. "The green one," he said. And so we got him a pistachio ice cream cone. It was a great moment. I didn't know the *Shehecheyanu* then. But if I did, I would have sung it. Our baby was having his first ice cream cone. He was getting well again.

The boys shared the bedroom next to ours. When they grew out of their cribs, we got them twin beds with a nightstand in between, and we had a long desk built beneath the windows for them to share. They always got along quite well, although they were very different. Arthur was more on the serious side. Michael was mischievous. Arthur seemed very cooperative, although there were times he'd agreed to do something and end up not doing it. Michael was the opposite. You would tell him to do something and he'd say "No!" Then often as not, he'd end up doing it anyway.

When they were still little, we spent summers at a farm in the Catskills owned by my cousin, Manny Feiner. Many years before, when he first came to the United States from Neustadt, Manny had lived with us in Port Chester. After he brought his wife over, he decided he wanted to own his own piece of land, something that was very rare for Jews in Europe, and he bought this farm in the Catskills. It was a typical farm with cows and chickens. But in the summer it doubled as the kind of boardinghouse unique to the Catskills, known as a *kochalayan*.

At the farm, Arthur used to content himself playing with the cows and running around in the fields, but Michael had to get into everything. At the end of each day he had acquired a bunch of splinters, which were so difficult to remove. And he loved to play in the dirt, which led to his getting impetigo. I spent hours scraping off the scabs, and Michael would go around covered in gentian violet.

When the boys were a little older, we began renting a summer bungalow at the Jacoby Bungalow Colony in Woodbourne. Television had begun to become very important around that time, and we brought up a little Philco. One day, I came into the living room to find Michael lying on the floor watching television. His big black eyes were wide open, and I could tell something was on his mind.

"Michael, what are you thinking about?" I asked.

"I was just wondering, when you and Dad die, who gets the television?" he said.

"We'll worry about that when the time comes," I told him.

From early on, we called Michael "the fixer." Just like his grandfather, this little kid was able to take anything apart and put it together again. If one part was left over and he didn't know what to do with it, he would just throw it out.

We were visiting Max and Ida one day when Michael was about six. Max was the kind of man who didn't like to get rid of things. Now he said to Michael, "I got a broken toaster. You wanna play with it?"

"Sure," said Michael. He sat on the floor and took the toaster apart. Then slowly but surely he put it together again. Max plugged it in the wall and to his delight, it worked!

Both Arthur and Michael were good students but never at the top of their class. When Michael was in the second or third grade at P.S. 207, he brought home a report card where the category "Shows little effort" was checked.

"Michael," I said, "you could be such a better student if you showed more effort."

He looked me straight in the eye. "But Mother, you don't understand," he said. "It doesn't say I show no effort. It says I do show effort. I show a little effort."

Now that I had children, my life centered around my home and neighborhood. Marine Park was on the outskirts of Flatbush, between Avenues S and T and the East 30s. It was a middle-class, white- and blue-collar neighborhood, and not primarily Jewish. Many of our neighbors were firemen and policemen. When my parents first bought the house, a golf course was supposed to be built nearby. It didn't come up until much later, but a large playground area for the kids was there all along, and the schools like P.S. 207 were wonderful. I wouldn't call Marine Park upscale, but it was a better area than most, with people who were not wealthy but substantial, who earned a good living and lived a good life.

One of my first and best friends in Marine Park was Eva Ezra, a tall, dark-haired, and very attractive woman whose husband was a lawyer and a Sephardic Jew. At first, his family felt his marrying Eva was tantamount to intermarriage. But she won them over very quickly.

Eva was forward, exuberant, a lover of life. She had everything under control; she could do it all. She could assess a person very quickly – sometimes right and sometimes wrong. If she didn't like you, forget it. You were out.

I thought her home was overkill. Too much of everything. Her choice of artwork was dreadful. But she was a wonderful hostess. No sooner did you sit down, when she'd begin to fry up some of her irresistible cheese latkes.

Her taste in clothes was horrible. Once, she came to a bar mitzvah dressed in the colors of a Christmas tree: a kelly green dress with bright red accessories. Later on she asked me, "How did you like the way I put the colors together?"

"Well, Eva," I said, "since you're asking me, I have to tell you. They weren't such a good combination."

"But you once wore something that was green and red," she cried.

"I know," I said, "but there are greens and there are reds."

Eva had never gone to college but she was well read and could discuss any current event. I think one of the things she liked about me was the fact that I was educated. She thought having a master's degree was pretty special. It was kind of unique at that time.

But Eva knew far more about sex than I did, and I learned a lot from her. Even after I was married I had a lot to learn. For the longest time I didn't know women had two separate openings: the vagina and the urethra.

As much as I cared for Eva, that's how little I cared for another neighbor, Adele. There were some who thought she was actually a witch. One of my friends went so far as to make certain to be wearing something red – a red pin, a red scarf, or a red hat, whenever Adele was around.

My one encounter with Adele, if you can call it that, came about after I had some major dental work. Inexplicably when I was still in my thirties, my four front teeth suddenly began to protrude. There was something wrong with my gums, and my upper teeth were rotting. I'd had such good healthy teeth. I couldn't believe they were going.

As luck would have it, I didn't have a good dentist at this time. Rivia's mother had died, and her father, Dr. Mishnoff, whom I loved like a father, had married his nurse. Then he did a terrible thing to me. He moved to the west coast with his new wife.

I tried out four different dentists. One had bad breath, another had a big belly that got in the way of everything he did, the third had an obnoxious personality, the fourth had dirt under his fingernails.

Finally Al said, "Why don't you go to Nadel's son?" Nadel was one of Al's clients. His son had just graduated from dental school with all the top honors.

"Go to a kid?" I said. "Absolutely not."

But then I got desperate and made an appointment with Al Nadel. I went into his office on Ocean Avenue, and immediately I fell in love with him. He was clean. His office was new and bright. I opened my mouth and felt good about giving it to him. He became my dentist, the dentist of my entire family, and of all my friends.

Now that I had found a dentist, I had to make a decision. Should I pull out all my top teeth and make a denture? The idea of it was terrible. Old people have dentures, not young people like me.

But together with Al Nadel, I decided that would be the best thing to do. I had a denture made, and I've been wearing it ever since.

I never advertised my dental problems, but somehow Adele found out about them. Her son Robert and Arthur were good friends. One day after they had been playing together, Arthur came running home. "Mommy, Mommy!" he cried. "Do you have false teeth?"

"What are you talking about?"

"Adele told me you didn't have your own teeth any more, that you're wearing false teeth, and you have to take them out at night."

"Well," I said, "you go back to Adele and tell her I said to wash her mouth out with a bar of soap."

I could never forgive her for saying such a thing to a child, even though I am a forgiving person, and even though I knew she had her own problems. She had the biggest bust I ever saw, so big she had to fold her breasts over in her brassiere. Also, she was envious of everyone and wasn't satisfied with her lot.

I, on the other hand, have always been satisfied with what I had. I have never envied anyone. In Marine Park, my life threw me into a nice community, but most of my friends were always one or two levels above me. I liked going to their professionally decorated homes, but then I'd come back to my house and say, "Hey, this is beautiful." I guess that was because I put so much of myself into my house, into the things I bought, the things I was given. It seemed to me some of my friends' homes had the decorator's look instead of theirs. I liked the idea of building a framework around me, of creating a home that represented what Al and I thought was important.

I was generally a satisfied person, happy with my home, my marriage and children, and my appearance as well. Except for the bump on my nose that I had first spotted on my wedding pictures. It only was noticeable in profile, but I began to study my profile, and the more I studied it, the more it bothered me. A nose job is so common nowadays. At that time, however, it was still very unusual. Still, I raised the subject with Al Fried. He was very kind. "Helen, I think you're beautiful. But if it bothers you, get rid of it," he said.

Well, now that I had his approval, I wasted no time in finding a plastic surgeon. I went into the city and had it done. When I came back, I told the kids that I fell getting off the bus, broke my nose, and had to have it fixed. The true story remained Al's and my secret.

In my life, my family came first. And in my family, my husband came first, then my kids, then my parents, and the rest. When I prepared food, I only prepared one meal, and that was what Al liked. And as a result, my boys grew up to eat almost everything. It was the opposite of how Eva handled cooking. She would make five different dishes for her four sons and her husband. Of course, my sons always wanted to eat at Eva's house.

As I look back on this period, I can say it was a good time – except that the first four years after I became a mother was the period of the Second World War. Everything was colored by that event, despite the fact that it didn't touch us directly. The men of draft age all got a number that determined when they would get called up. Fortunately for us, Al got a very late number, and the war ended before it was reached. No one in my immediate family was in the army. How lucky we were.

Still, I would feel uncomfortable with friends whose husbands or sweethearts were fighting in the war. Many of the men and boys in the neighborhood were away, and not all came back. There was one young man named Joe Berlin, a short guy with a smile that made you think the whole world was great. I remembered how quick he was; he could get out of anything. But he didn't get out of the war.

We heard terrible things were happening to the Jews in Europe, but no one could imagine the reality. Once, we went to hear a lecture by Rabbi Stephen Wise, and he described such Nazi atrocities as making soap out of people. I simply couldn't believe the things he said were possible.

Still, I knew I had to get involved in Jewish causes. I thought I would join Hadassah. Its focus on Zionism appealed to me, and there was a group that met on Kings Highway, which wasn't too far away. But when I mentioned it to my father, he said, "No. I don't think you should do that. You should join Mama's group, the Ladies' Auxiliary at the *shul*."

I was surprised. Papa wasn't a Sabbath observer. He wasn't active in the Marine Park synagogue, a small storefront *shul* on Avenue S, near East Thirty-fourth Street that barely got a daily *minyan* together. The Ladies' Auxiliary was made up of a handful of women of my mother's generation, and the only thing they did, as far as I could see, was raise money for the synagogue by having a bazaar.

But if my father asked me to do something, I couldn't refuse. I put Hadassah on hold and joined the Ladies' Auxiliary. It turned out to be one of the key decisions of my life.

V

BRANCHING OUT

I BEGAN GOING ALONG WITH MAMA to the meetings of her Ladies' Auxiliary, where ten or twelve middle-aged to elderly women would sit around and talk about how to raise money, raise money, raise money. Sitting through those meetings, my mind would drift back to the time I taught Sunday School at my grandfather's synagogue in Bay Ridge. Even though I was just a teenager then, I was aware of how busy a place it was, how the women, as much as the men, were always showing up for lectures and study groups. The atmosphere was so enlightening. Here in Marine Park, I heard no discussion about what was going on in the world, about what was happening to the Jews in Europe, about Zionism or Jewish tradition and history. The women were nice enough, but nothing they were doing seemed uplifting to me.

Then, a few months after I joined, I was offered the post of presidency. It came as a total surprise. The women were all much older than I was. I must have seemed like a kid to them. But they seemed so very eager for me to take up their offer that I gave it some serious thought. If I were to become president, I would have to find a way to make this a more interesting group.

Someone had told me about the National Women's League, the central body of ladies' auxiliaries from Conservative synagogues, and now I made it my business to find out what it was about. Women's League, I learned, was founded in 1918 by Mathilde Schechter, the widow of Solomon Schechter, who had founded the parent body of the Conservative movement: United

Synagogues of America. Henrietta Szold, the founder of Hadassah, was one of its original members. The organization had branches all over the United States, Canada, and even Mexico, and its purpose was to strengthen Jewish knowledge and values through programs and courses in how to read Hebrew, understand the Bible, and participate in the holidays. It also provided methods for organizing women's groups. And all that was required for affiliation was the payment of dues – twenty-five cents a member.

This is great, I thought. This is how you build up a ladies' auxiliary.

I reported back to the women, confident they would think I was presenting them with a wonderful gift. But when I mentioned the dues, they threw up their hands. "What? Twenty-five cents from each of us?" They wouldn't hear of it.

I, however, was very, very determined. "Well, if you can't do it, I can't be the president," I said. There followed a long and heated discussion, the upshot of which was they relented.

Having surmounted that hurdle and with our auxiliary now a member of Women's League, I was now faced with the challenge of enhancing our membership. Marine Park had changed from the time my parents had bought their house. Many young families had moved into the neighborhood; there were more professional people. I wanted to get the younger women involved in our organization, but I didn't know which or how many were Jewish. My next-door neighbors, as well as those living directly across the way and behind me, were gentile.

Then I came up with the idea of canvassing the community on foot. I enlisted the help of Eva Ezra, and together we pushed our baby carriages up and down the blocks, stopping to look at the nameplates on the houses. If a name sounded Jewish, we'd ring the doorbell. If a young woman came to the door, we'd introduce ourselves and tell her about the new organization that was forming at the synagogue. We underscored the fact that it was a social thing, a way to meet other young women. Often that was the chief selling point. But we also stressed how our organization would enhance their knowledge of the beautiful traditions of Jewish life.

If Eva and I heard about someone new who had moved into the community, we would stop by on a Friday with a *challah* and bottle of wine, a gift expressing *Shabbat Shalom*. Often we were successful, but sometimes we made mistakes. Like the time we rang the bell of Mrs. Lehman. She was most pleasant, even invited us inside. But after we told her what we were about she said, "Oh, but I'm not Jewish."

But then there was the time we opened the gate of a white picket fence and rang the doorbell of Charlotte Levine who had just moved into "the house of my dreams," as she put it.

After listening to our spiel, the very young and very pregnant Charlotte said, "Your organization sounds appealing. But I'm new to the neighborhood, and I don't think I'm ready to join an organization right away. Besides," she added, "I've just committed myself to a group that will be learning to play mah-jongg."

"Oh, but we teach mah-jongg too," I said impulsively. Mah-jongg was very popular in those days. I was an excellent player, and since I had already taught piano, Sunday School, and typing, I was confident I could teach anything – even mah-jongg.

Charlotte wavered. "In that case…"

As soon as I got home that afternoon, I corralled a group and got Charlotte into it. Mah-jongg classes turned out to be a regular offering that first year when we were building up our membership. We lured more than a few ladies through the game. But as I got to know Charlotte, who soon became my second best friend in Marine Park, I realized she would have joined our organization with or without the mah-jongg. She was the daughter of a cantor, and her growing up years in Chelsea, Massachusetts, had been rich in Jewish life.

Charlotte was the exception in that respect. Most of our new members had had very little to do with Judaism. But once they got involved, their interest was sparked. Through the guidance of Women's League, we learned how to organize our group into an effective body. They sent materials. They held conferences, and I attended every one that I possibly could. I didn't miss a thing.

We began a lecture series. We set up a weekly meeting with the rabbi, devoted to Bible study, often discussing the *Torah* portion of the week and applying it to current events. One session I remember very well was devoted to the Book of Job and its connection to the Holocaust, which was just beginning to be talked about at the time. These were serious discussions. In most cases the women were up to it. And if they weren't, they sat there as if they knew what was going on.

It took a little more than a year for the membership and direction of Mama's Ladies' Auxiliary to be transformed by the addition of at least twenty-five new members and a range of educational and social offerings. There were some difficulties at first when some of the older members felt they were being put on the shelf. But I appointed a few of them to the executive committee, and they began to appreciate the fact that their auxiliary was becoming a different kind of women's organization with new programming, a new ideology, and a new name: the Sisterhood of the Marine Park Jewish Center.

The change in name was most appropriate, as we were an auxiliary of nothing. Typically in synagogues, the men's organizations lead the way. In the Marine Park Jewish Center, the sisterhood was the spearhead. It was the women who got their husbands involved. Most of the men had been bar mitzvahed years before and that was it. But now they too were becoming active.

We developed a vital social program. We raised money by staging versions of popular Broadway shows, like *Guys and Dolls*, changing the lyrics to make them apply to our world. They were the corniest things but still the social events of the year.

The Marine Park Jewish Center had taken off. Still, it was housed in the storefront locale with one large room that served as sanctuary and social hall, a kitchen, and a small office. Then, one evening at a crowded fund-raising event, Eva, who was carrying a tray with hot dogs, suddenly fell right through the floor to the basement beneath. Apparently she had stepped on a weak spot. It was a miracle that she wasn't hurt. But this was a sign that a new building for the synagogue had to be put at the top of our list of priorities. Our fund-raising efforts were increased and, before long, the synagogue was housed in a handsome new edifice.

From its inception, the Marine Park Jewish Center was Conservative in approach, even though it was founded as an Orthodox synagogue and never officially joined the Conservative movement. Before I became active, I never gave much thought to its style of worship. Afterwards, my grandfather's influence prompted me to steer it in the direction of Conservative Judaism. However, in all the years we were part of the congregation, we could never get a Conservative rabbi. I guess there weren't that many around back then, and our temple was not that prominent. Also, we couldn't afford to pay a very high salary. As a result, all our rabbis were

Orthodox. And in those days, when an Orthodox rabbi took a position in a Conservative synagogue, he viewed it as his duty to try to convert it to more Orthodox practices.

Rabbi Abraham Besdin was the rabbi when my children were growing up. He was a brilliant man, but not right for a Conservative synagogue. Several times he tried unsuccessfully to get the men and women to sit in separate sections. He was successful, however, in steering the kids to the youth groups of his choice. This was very upsetting to me. I wanted to see them join the youth programs of the Conservative movement, like USY (United Synagogue Youth) and Camp Ramah. He said, "I couldn't allow the young people to belong to such organizations." I had come up against the proverbial stone wall. It reminded me of the time Rabbi Ginsburg had thrown me out of the *Talmud Torah* in Port Chester so many years before.

This time, however, Mama sided with me. She was very proud of my accomplishments with the sisterhood. I think it was the first example of her seeing me in action. I was also active in the P.T.A of P.S. 207; I went on to join Hadassah. I always seemed to have time for everything; I don't know how.

Al and I had a wonderful social life with people in the neighborhood. We were part of a group of six couples who would get together once a month in each other's homes. The men would play poker, the women canasta or mah-jongg. All the winnings would go into a pot, and when there was enough, we'd go to places like Jamaica or Bermuda for a little vacation.

Lillian and Henry Ruderman and Lillian's sister, Renee, and her husband, Martin Cutler, who actually lived in Bensonhurst, were two of the couples in the group. Both Henry and Martin were doctors – a very prestigious profession in those days. Lillian was an artist and an excellent piano player. It was interesting how many of the women I knew back then played the piano. We had taken lessons as kids, and pianos had places of honor in our living rooms.

Then there was Isabel and Harry Josephsberg. Harry was an importer of giftware from Japan, and the Josephsbergs often went to Tokyo on buying trips. Later on, through my assistance, Isabel would become vice president of Women's League. She was an attractive woman, outgoing and personable. But when I learned she had never graduated from the college in Philadelphia she claimed to have attended, that the picture of her purported college graduation was actually taken when she graduated from high school, my feelings towards her cooled.

Of course Eva and Morris Ezra and Charlotte and Nathan Levine were part of the group. Charlotte was very attractive and always beautifully dressed. Nathan manufactured plastic packaging way ahead of everyone else. He did extremely well, and before long, they moved to a tremendous house in Woodmere, Long Island, with a beautiful garden. But we remained lifelong friends.

One night early on in our friendship, we were leaving Eva Ezra's house after a card-playing session. There was snow on the ground, the steps outside the house were icy, and Charlotte was heavily pregnant with her first child. "I plan to have five children," she declared, as we struggled to get her down the stairs.

"Humph!" I thought. "You haven't got one yet." I had two and was having problems – Arthur with his digestive tract, Michael with celiac – and here was this woman, trying with difficulty and a good deal of help from us to make it safely down a few steps, announcing she was going to have five children.

Well, she did – four girls and one boy!

I almost had three. When my boys were about five and seven, I discovered I was pregnant. Al Fried and I struggled over whether I should go through with the pregnancy. We realized another child would make our situation very difficult. We weighed the costs of education later on, which was always foremost in our minds. Yet I kept thinking maybe this was the girl I had always wanted.

Finally we decided that it wouldn't be wise for us to have another child. I began inquiring among the women I knew, telling them a friend of mine needed an abortion. It was not until I was in my third month that I finally found a doctor who would do it.

Al and I went to his office, a dingy-looking place on the bottom floor of a tenement building in downtown Brooklyn. Al waited outside while I walked into the operating room. I looked around and saw all these instruments and metal pans where the fetuses were deposited. Everything looked so dirty to me. "What am I doing?" I asked myself. "Am I killing this little girl in me?"

Three other women were there. We were all lined up. The doctor gave me a lot of attention, feeling me all over, groping my breasts. But I was afraid if I told him to stop, I would anger him and he wouldn't go ahead and do this thing.

Afterwards, I never shared this experience with anyone but Al. At the same time, I never forgot it. The emotional pain stayed with me for years.

Just around the time I would have had my third child, my friend Lillian Winston gave birth to her son, Paul. I would see Paul and think, "Look what I have done. And mine would have been a girl." But after a while, I changed my mind. "Oh well, more than likely it would have been a boy," I'd say to myself.

During the years I was busy building up the sisterhood, Al was busy building up his private accounting practice. At first, his connection to the synagogue was largely through me. But then his mother died, and for the next eleven months he said *kaddish* at the synagogue twice a day. As a result, he became very close to the Marine Park Jewish Center and ultimately served as its president.

Even before he became president, Al was a generous donor, albeit an anonymous one. Unlike the others, he would never allow his name and the amount of his donation to be called out in the synagogue. I would have the biggest quarrels with him. "If people like the Meisels or Weisses [some of the richer congregants] hear how much you're giving – whether it's a hundred dollars or three hundred dollars – maybe they'll give more," I'd tell him. But to no avail. Both Arthur and Michael, who went on to become generous contributors with long lists of causes, continue their father's tradition of anonymous giving to this day.

The death of my mother-in-law was a big blow to us. Al was very devoted to her; I also loved her. Despite her loss, we continued the tradition of Sunday afternoon visits to the family home in Bensonhurst where his father, his sister Lee and her husband lived. Al had a big, close family – four sisters and one brother, and on Sundays all of them, with spouses and children, would get together. Arthur and Michael would play stickball or punchball with their cousins out on the street, even though they were dressed in their visiting clothes, while the grown-ups spent the afternoon drinking tea and talking.

We didn't have to visit my parents, since we continued living with them. Often people would ask me, "How is it working out, living together with your mother and father?" And I couldn't understand why they asked, because to me, it always seemed so correct. I think my sons grew up as well as they did because they learned to appreciate the values of an older person. Al and my father were particularly close. To live in a house together, to share a bathroom for all those years, you have to be close.

Strangely enough, my parents had not suffered during the Depression. At first, Uncle Max's knitting mill continued to do well. When it began to falter, my father went into the buttonhole manufacturing business and made a success of it. Later on, however, times became more difficult. During the war, there was a rash of foreclosures in the neighborhood because people couldn't meet their mortgage payments, and my parents were among those in danger of losing their homes.

At that time, we had the chance to buy a semi-attached house across the street that was about to be foreclosed. Mama suggested we buy into their house instead. "Half the house will be yours, and in case anything should happen to us, you'll own it entirely," she said. It made sense.

Because we had been living with my parents for so many years, contributing modestly every month, we were able to save, and now we had enough money to buy our share of the house. Eight was always a fixed number in my mind, eight from eighteen, or *chai* – the numeration of the Hebrew word that means life. We waited until we had eight thousand dollars in the bank before we started a family. Now we paid eight thousand dollars to my mother and were half owners of the house.

With half the house belonging to Al and me, I felt free to redecorate. I replaced the old living room couch with a new couch and a loveseat. Al had procured some very fine material from one of his clients in shades of purple, light turquoise, and green, and we used it to make drapery for the living and dining rooms.

Naturally, I kept the beautiful baby grand piano that my mother and I had bought together before I was married. Papa would never buy anything on the installment plan; he had to pay cash up front. But I had convinced my mother back then to buy a piano together with me in installments. Even though she was a very strong person, my mother usually went along with whatever I wanted.

I think the women in my family were stronger than the men. My father was more passive, my mother more controlling. With Al, I was stronger in some ways, but in other ways I would defer to him out of my love for him. He could get angry quickly but he cooled down very fast. Somehow, instinctively, I knew how to make it with him.

My drive, my ability to go after what I wanted, came from my mother. She knew what she wanted to do and did it. I remember how she would take a letter and extrapolate certain words and use them in letters that she wrote. I remember her creating her own English dictionary. Sometimes she used the words correctly and sometimes not.

Our living together was a good arrangement all around. We got along so well, at least I thought so. I don't know how my mother felt, but my father would have been heartsick if we hadn't stayed in the house with them, because he loved being with us and the kids.

I tried not to lay too much babysitting on my mother. Of course, at night my parents would be home, and as I became more and more active and had many meetings to attend, that was a great help to me. Also, we weren't together all the time, as I went away with the children every summer, first to the Catskills and later on to the Berkshires.

Most of the people in Marine Park sent their children to sleepaway camps, but we wanted to spend the summers with the boys in a proper kind of setting, and the Jacoby Bungalow Colony in Woodbourne provided just that. It had an excellent day camp run by Mr. Wegman, who was the head of the Woodbourne school system. He learned a lot about Jewish kids through his day camp, and the Jewish kids learned a lot about him.

Mr. Jacoby – somehow no matter how well we knew him, he always remained Mr. Jacoby – was a strong guy who did everything correctly; he was a terrific proprietor. At the beginning of each season he would say to me, "Helen, I hope you don't mind. I want to take some people through your bungalow." I think that was because my bungalow was the most attractive of all. I would take the kids out of school early each summer to get up there and fix up the place.

Jacoby's daughter-in-law, Arlene, was my good friend. I liked her a lot. She was different from anyone else I knew. Most of the women at the colony were pretty organized. Arlene wasn't. Keeping a neat and tidy house wasn't one of her priorities. When you walked into her house, you had to step over five thousand things before you got to see her pretty face. But that was because she was involved in so many other things. She was artistic; she was up on things that were going on. She was well read, well educated. Not many of the women at the bungalow colony were college graduates. Arlene was.

Jacoby's had its own rituals. Early each morning, the bell would ring:

clang, clang, clang, as Benjy, the bakery delivery man, drove up in his little van. He'd slide the door open and all the women would run out to get their fresh rolls, breads, and cakes. Somehow, Benjy always seemed to favor me over the others. Even if I came out a little later, he'd turn to wait on me, putting a few of the crisp rolls that I loved into a bag along with a couple of Danishes for the kids.

"Why are you always paying more attention to her? Why do you take her first?" the other women would ask.

Benjy didn't answer, but I knew why. Before I went out, I had put on lipstick and maybe a little powder. I had combed my hair; I was wearing a nice robe. I wasn't prettier than the others, but I took the trouble to make myself look good, while they generally looked no better than an unmade bed. Benjy and I had a good relationship. I'd always stop to chat with him, and in this way, I always got his attention.

All week long Al worked in the city. But when he drove up on Friday evenings, his car filled with other husbands who got a ride with him, it was hallelujah. Saturday and Sunday afternoons he'd go off to the big hotels to play golf. He was always an avid golfer.

I was without the car during the week, but everything we needed was close at hand. There was the day camp for the kids, the swimming pool, the main house where the Borscht Circuit comedians, singers, and novelty acts would appear on Saturday nights. We also put on our own shows. Once, I played the part of a mermaid and made a costume out of a slithery green gown with little plastic drop beads that I had bought at Russek's some years before. I used a mop that I dyed a bright shade of yellow for my hair and was wheeled onstage reclining on a beach lounge.

The big event of the season was our midsummer masquerade party. People were so creative. I remember a guy named Jerry who played Toulouse-Lautrec. He got the idea from the movie *Moulin Rouge*, which was popular then. When he walked in, nobody could figure out who he really was. As the flower lady, I was easier to recognize. Dressed in a black dress with a little black hat, I walked around saying, "Violets please? Five cents. Violets please?"

These years of my life were filled with the typical pleasures and routines of being a young wife and mother, but they were enormously enhanced by my involvement with our sisterhood, and subsequently with its parent organization, Women's League.

As president of the Sisterhood of the Marine Park Jewish Center, I was invited to the meetings of the Metropolitan Branch of Women's League that represented the five boroughs of New York City and the surrounding suburbs. The first meeting I went to was at Temple Beth El of Manhattan Beach, and it was there that I first met the presidents of other sisterhoods. Many were teachers. A few were lawyers. Some had gone to Jewish day school and knew how to *daven*. All were educated and informed. I was so impressed with them.

After that, I attended every meeting of the Metropolitan Branch that I possibly could, always sitting up front, trying not to miss a thing. In the process, I learned parliamentary procedure and how to conduct a more orderly meeting. I learned about interesting programming and fund-raising concepts, and met speakers whom I invited to our sisterhood to deliver lectures about the struggle for Israeli statehood, Jewish history, and ways to enhance Jewish life in the home.

Being active in the local branch brought me to the attention of the executive branch of Women's League, and soon I was invited to sit in on national meetings. There I met some extraordinary women who would have an enormous impact on me. There was Fannie Minkin, the wife of a professor at the Jewish Theological Seminary and an important figure in Women's League. Fannie had no children; I was like her bright little daughter, and she communicated to me her enthusiasm for learning and Judaism.

Sarah Kopelman was president around the time I became active. She was an attorney, a handsome, tall, and attractive woman, not bubbly but cultured and erudite. Sarah initiated the Social Action Committee of Women's League, which propelled the organization into taking positions and advocating in areas like civil rights and civil liberties.

Sarah lived opposite the Park Avenue Synagogue and towards the end of her life, I would visit her whenever I had the chance. By this time, she was blind. "I wrote you a letter last night," she'd say to me. "Do you want me to tell you about it?" And she would go on and recount what she would have liked to say in the letter she had thought about but was unable to write. Her daughter was married to a leading ophthalmologist, and I used to wonder, why can't this great eye doctor help his mother-in-law see again?

Although I was not really ready, not trained, I was picked up quickly by women like Fannie, Sarah, and Helen Sussman, another exceptional leader, who would become president some years after Sarah and who radiated enormous energy and electricity. They all sensed my interest in the organization and my willingness to prepare myself to do whatever would be needed.

In 1948 I was invited to be a delegate to the National Convention that was held in Atlantic City. This, my first convention, was most auspicious, as it took place the year Israel became a state.

I took my mother and Al's sister, Ida, along with me. As soon as we arrived, I telephoned home. Al answered the phone.

"How's everything?" I asked.

"Everything's fine," he said, but I could hear Michael sniffling in the background.

"Let me talk to Michael."

He got on the phone sobbing, "Where are you? When are you coming home?"

I felt so terrible hearing him cry. But I made up my mind there and then, when I go away and I know my kids are safe and well, I won't talk to them while I'm gone. And I kept that vow until they were grown.

The convention was a big event in my life to that point. Twelve hundred delegates were present. So many events were going on, it was mind-boggling. An election was going to be held, which was most unusual. As a rule, the choices of the nominating committee were not contested, but in this case, Mrs. Kavey, a very bright and forceful woman, arranged to be nominated as vice president from the floor.

Ironically, I knew Mrs. Kavey. I remembered her from Port Chester, where she was the president of the local bank. Now, as she went around campaigning, my mother noticed her. She was so delighted to see someone she recognized that she called out to her, "Mrs. Kavowitz, Mrs. Kavowitz."

"My name is Kavey now," Mrs. Kavey said.

Later on, when I became president of Women's League, Mrs. Kavey would tell me, "I thought when you became president, you would use me more." I felt bad that she believed she was being excluded, because she was such a willing participant, and we were grateful for her extensive contributions. She was the one who brought the plight of Ethiopian Jews to our attention.

Now that I was becoming more and more active in the Metropolitan Branch, my geographical world expanded to include Morningside Heights, where the Women's League office was located, within the Jewish Theological Seminary on 122nd Street and Broadway. That part of the city was so unfamiliar to me. I was struck by the hilly landscape and the neo-Georgian buildings of the Seminary and nearby Columbia University and Barnard College. The area didn't look like Brooklyn at all.

The first time I walked through the Seminary's towering gates, I passed a tall and thin man with a small beard. "My goodness," I thought. "He looks just like Jesus."

"Who is that?" I asked a woman beside me.

"Oh, don't you know? It's Rabbi Louis Finkelstein, the chancellor."

I felt like running over to introduce myself. Of course, I didn't. But in the years to come, I would get to know Rabbi Finkelstein very well.

I'd also get to hear many stories about him, like the time he was in the elevator of the Seminary with a group of people. With his typical courtesy, he asked each person where he or she was going and pressed the appropriate floor button. Two gentile visitors happened to be in the elevator at that time. One turned to the other and said, "In this place, even the elevator operators wear beards."

The Jewish Theological Seminary could be called the Vatican of Conservative Jewry. It was the central body of the movement where Conservative rabbis were trained and ordained. Back then, there were no female rabbis, but many of the students at the Seminary were women studying to be teachers in synagogues and Jewish day schools. Women's League was a major fund-raising source for the Seminary, and the Seminary in turn was a source for Women's League members to learn more about Judaism.

As my Jewish education had been so limited, I now tried as best as I could to enhance my knowledge. It still angered me to think back to the time I followed my brother, Hy, to Hebrew school and was thrown out because I was a girl. I felt I had so much to make up for.

I never learned to speak Hebrew, but I did learn to recognize the letters so I could follow the services in a *siddur*. I attended every lecture and study group I could manage, always arriving ahead of time, always up front in the very first row.

At the Seminary, I met distinguished leaders of Conservative Judaism, people who would have a tremendous influence on my life and from whom I would learn so much. It was from Rabbi Max Artz, the father of Mim Teplitz, who was to become my good friend, that I learned that on Friday nights the father blesses his children. I had not known about this beautiful and meaningful ceremony before, but now I asked Al if he would do it. Of course, he agreed. It became part of our Friday night ritual, and today my sons and grandchildren continue the tradition with their children.

The Conservative movement had experienced tremendous growth during this postwar period. As people moved out to the suburbs and new neighborhoods within the cities, the number of synagogues increased. While, on the one hand, the synagogue remained the vehicle through which people reached God, participated in rituals, and were exposed to the treasures of Judaism, it had also become the instrument for establishing and maintaining a social life in a new community. Beyond these factors, the realization of how much of the Jewish world had been destroyed during the war made people want to be proactive in their Jewishness.

By the 1950s there were so many new Conservative synagogues in the New York region that the Metropolitan Branch of Women's League became too large and unwieldy. It was decided to break it up into various branches for different suburban regions and boroughs. Brooklyn, with thirty sister-hoods and a total membership of 4,500, was deemed large and active enough to be a branch of its own. In 1952 I became its first president.

Shortly before I took over and while Brooklyn was still what was called a branch-in-training, I was put on the three-woman planning committee for the *Torah* Fund luncheon. *Torah* Fund is a major Seminary fund-raising effort on the part of Women's League. At that time, a minimum contribu-tion of $6.11 – the numerical value of the word *Torah* is 611 – enabled a sisterhood member to be part of this group and attend a gala luncheon. This year it would be held at the Pierre Hotel on Fifth Avenue. The cost was four dollars a person.

I felt very important to be on this committee, working with women who represented top leadership and were quite a bit older than I was. Many years later, my granddaughter Rachel would be married at the Pierre, but back then I wasn't used to going to such places.

When we went to meet with one of the hotel vice presidents, I dressed with particular care. I no longer had the time to sew as much of my ward-robe as I once did, but I still made all my own hats, relying on the skills I had picked up as a teenager working at the Jonas Millinery Shop long ago. This time, I came up with a lavender felt head band crowned with a veil that went well with the Shrader suit I had bought in a slightly deeper shade. So attired, I felt very comfortable meeting with the Pierre's vice president to plan the luncheon and select a kosher caterer from their list.

Alyce Platek was one of the Metropolitan Branch leaders who recognized my potential and helped me move on to positions of greater responsibility. After attending meetings in each other's homes, we discovered we had something in common. Both of us served Ebinger's cake, and both of us had sons who loved Ebinger's cake. Alyce's son, Stanley – who would go on to become a distinguished rabbi – and Michael would be the first kids home from school whenever they knew a Metropolitan Branch meeting was being held at home. It got to the point where I had to hide the cake in the body of my baby grand piano to keep Michael from getting at it before the ladies arrived.

When I became president of the brand new Brooklyn Branch, I felt it was a great accomplishment not only for myself, but for the Marine Park Jewish Center. After all, compared with the many major congregations like the Brooklyn Jewish Center on Eastern Parkway, the East Midwood Jewish Center in Flatbush, or Temple Emanuel in Borough Park, we were modest, more like the new kid on the block. It was kind of ironic that the first president of Brooklyn Branch came out of this upstart synagogue. But as I had done with the Sisterhood of Marine Park, I was determined to put Brooklyn Branch on the map.

It was a full-time job with a lot of administrative and development work. We created a strong social action program. I began lecturing at sisterhoods throughout Brooklyn on the Seminary and the values of Judaism.

Every Women's League convention and every branch conference had a theme based on a biblical quotation. The first Brooklyn Branch conference, which was held at the East Midwood Jewish Center, had the theme "Let There Be Light." Our goal was to shed light on the members of our sisterhoods in terms of Jewish living and learning.

At one point, I invited Rabbi Abraham Joshua Heschel to come and speak to us. He was still a relative newcomer, but his first book had been critically acclaimed, and everyone thought of him as up and coming. When he originally came to this country from Germany, he was a refugee from Hitler's fascism. Although still a young man, he already had a reputation as a scholar and was quickly picked up by the Reform movement to teach at Hebrew Union College in Cincinnati. But since he was very observant, he wasn't happy there, and before long he moved over to the Seminary.

That was where I picked him up. He was very young, probably in his late thirties, cosmopolitan and very polite, with dark black hair and piercing eyes that looked right at you when he spoke to you. He spoke with a heavy accent, and I had to pay careful attention to understand what he was saying.

As we drove down to Brooklyn, he questioned me about the women's group. "Do most of the women have a kosher house?" he asked.

What could I say? Most did not. "Well, some of them do. But I'm not exactly certain who is and who isn't because I haven't been in all the homes. Among my friends, most keep kosher."

"Well...," was all he said.

That day, Rabbi Heschel spoke about the portion of the week, applying it to the audience. And although the women found it difficult to understand his accent, his personality shone through. He was so modest, so real. There was an unmistakable aura about him. Over the years, his speech improved tremendously and he became a well-known public figure and an activist who was widely quoted in matters dealing with theology, ethics, and morality.

One of the things I was especially proud of initiating during my presidency of Brooklyn Branch was our involvement in the work of the Jewish Braille Institute. I encouraged sisterhood members to take the Institute's course, which prepared them to transcribe *Torah* portions into braille. Many women throughout the country and Canada enrolled and subsequently went through the painstaking transcription process. Among those who made use of their labors was Michael Levy, a blind boy who prepared for his bar mitzvah with the braille our women had transcribed. He went on to become a rabbi, and remains active in the Jewish Braille Institute to this day.

Aside from my family, Women's League had become my great passion. I was part of that mid-century generation of middle-class women who did not work and found outlets for their talents and energies in volunteer organizational work. As a result of my father's suggestion, I had become immersed in an extraordinary organization that was enriching my life immeasurably.

Naturally, it took up a great deal of my time. Every so often, when I was rushing off to a meeting or over my head in planning some event, I would turn to my father and say, "Papa, look what you got me into."

He'd smile that quiet, gentle smile I loved so much. "Well, it was the right thing to do, wasn't it?" he'd say.

One day a few months before Arthur's bar mitzvah, my father called me into his bedroom. "I have something to show you," he said. He took a small box out of the dresser drawer and opened it. Inside was a handsome Hamilton watch set against a bed of black velvet. "It's my gift for Arthur," he said to me.

Sitting beside him on his bed holding the watch, I was reminded of the time he told us how he had asked his brother, Max, for his old watch only to be turned down. Now he was able to buy such a fine new watch for his grandson. My eyes filled up, and I embraced him. "Papa, it's beautiful," I said. "Arthur will love it."

Some days later, I was at the dressing table in the bathroom getting ready for bed when suddenly there was a knock on the door. "Helen, I have to come in," my father cried. I opened the door. He rushed over to the sink and began spitting up blood. There was so much blood, it was overflowing. I dashed downstairs to get a pan from the kitchen, returned to the bathroom, and shut the door behind me. My mother came running to see what was going on, but I wouldn't let her into the bathroom. I didn't want her to see this.

When I realized there was nothing I could do, I called Dr. Ruderman. He was sleeping already, but he got up and came over right away. "Your father is dying," he said to me. He explained that the blood wasn't going through the normal channels; it was just spurting out. By now, the bleeding had slowed down, and Papa was just limp.

I couldn't accept it. "You've got to get him to the hospital," I cried.

We got an ambulance and rushed him to the hospital. He died that same night.

Again I kept my mother away from him. I felt I was protecting her. But as we gathered outside his room once it was over, she said in Yiddish, "Even at his last moment I couldn't be with him."

That comment puzzled me so. What did she mean, I wondered. Why did she say "*Even* at his last moment?" Did it have something to do with my being with him at the end instead of her? Did she think I had taken over control of everything? Did she resent me?

VI

PREPARING FOR THE PRESIDENCY

We were still feeling my father's absence at Arthur's bar mitzvah. But Arthur did splendidly. All day long Mama had a smile from ear to ear. And the party was a rather lavish affair at the synagogue, which by then was second home to us. So it was a very happy day.

Papa's death was the first great loss of my life, and one way I dealt with it was by throwing myself into Women's League activities more than ever. When my two-year term as president of Brooklyn Branch ended in 1954, I moved onto the national board, becoming membership chair, then corresponding secretary, and ultimately one of twelve vice presidents before taking over the presidency in 1962.

I was coming into prominence in Jewish life in a very pivotal time, being part of a new generation of American Jewish women who had become emboldened to assert their Jewishness in the wake of the Holocaust and the creation of the State of Israel. If you had the interest and ability, it was possible to progress very fast in Women's League, and that was what was happening to me.

The more experienced women in the organization gave leadership training courses, of which I avidly availed myself, and before long I was asked to give courses myself. My first assignment was local, at the Brooklyn Jewish Center on Eastern Parkway. It was a little unnerving because I knew some of the women on its executive board – one was the mother of Harold Kushner (who went on to become world famous with his book *When Bad Things Happen to Good People*) – and they were more knowledgeable

Judaically than I. But as soon as I felt reciprocity from the group, a response you must establish very early on in the communications encounter, I got over any sense of insecurity.

Then I was sent out to work with sisterhood women in places throughout the country, in Canada, and in Mexico. As a rule, there would be about twenty to thirty women who had shown leadership potential. They would come together in a synagogue classroom, and over the course of two or three days I would lecture and lead discussions, the idea being that the women would then impart what they learned to the women in their congregations. In this way, I found myself back in front of a class, teaching once again.

Such experiences led to my giving leadership training and public speaking courses outside of Women's League as well. One that I recall in particular was to the members of the Bridge, an organization designed to help young people who had "strayed" for some reason, such as a girl who had gotten pregnant or a boy who was taking drugs, which was a rarity in those days. The Bridge's members were all doctors' wives and therefore in a position to reach such young people, helping them get proper medical and psychological treatment.

The ladies who belonged to the Bridge didn't need help in fund-raising; they were doing very well in that department, but they did need to improve their organizational and public speaking skills. So at our first meeting, after delivering my usual opening lecture on how to organize more efficiently and how to determine the responsibilities of officers, I handed out assignments for an "off-the-cuff" speech, just to make sure I knew what I was working with. Then I presented a selection of subjects that dealt with a current issue, such as the McCarthy hearings, which were going on at that time. The women picked a topic, and over the course of the week they prepared the speech they would present at our next meeting.

The most accomplished speaker from this group turned out to be the hostess of our first meeting. I remember when I entered her apartment on Montgomery Street how overwhelmed I was by its stunning décor. Clearly a very accomplished decorator had been at work here, I thought, one who knew her fabrics, colors, and accessories and was able to combine them to spectacular effect at no small cost.

After the session, our hostess called her maid, who had set a most elegant table with beautiful china and flatware. I could only imagine what would come next. And what came, on a magnificent sterling silver tray, was an assortment of package cookies: Lorna Doones, Oreos, and Mallomars. "It took me seven years of psychoanalysis to be able to serve these cookies to all of you," she said. We all laughed, certain she was joking, and waited. But that was it.

In addition to leadership training courses, I began giving private lessons in public speaking after Dr. Klein, a dentist in the neighborhood who had heard me speak as Sisterhood president, asked me to help him prepare an address for a dental conference. He spread the word and before I knew it, I was getting more requests for one-on-one training in speech and presentational skills than I could handle.

Beyond all these activities, I had become involved in the Social Action Committee of Women's League, particularly in the area of civil rights. My involvement coincided with the 1954 Supreme Court ruling that found unconstitutional the "separate but equal" doctrine that had kept many schools segregated, as well as the 1955 bus boycott in Montgomery, Alabama, that first brought Dr. Martin Luther King, Jr. to national prominence.

Somehow the cause of civil rights had always been close to my heart, although my sole personal contact with African Americans to that point in time had been my friend Lenore from Textile High School, with whom I'd lost touch years ago. The only other blacks I knew were the housekeepers most of us hired to clean our homes. It would always upset me whenever I heard them referred to as *shvartzes* ("black ones") in a generally pejorative sense. "Don't say that," I'd tell the women who used the term. "You should be grateful to these ladies who help us with the heavy housework."

I took it upon myself to help make the women in the various branches of Women's League aware of the civil rights movement. I felt very strongly that it was my responsibility as a Jewish woman. Judaism specifically teaches, "Justice, justice shall thou pursue,"* and there was no justice for so many African Americans.

Through our Social Action Committee I helped write "Alerts," one-page flyers that we would send out to the membership, informing them of what was going on, urging them to write to their congressmen and senators to support civil rights actions and to work for passage of a civil rights bill.

I found a kindred spirit in this cause with Rabbi Heschel, who was a great supporter and ally of Martin Luther King, Jr. He was on the front

---

* Deuteronomy 16:20.

line beside him for many of the marches and demonstrations and once introduced him to the New York Board of Rabbis as being out of the tradition of the prophets in the Bible.

From time to time, Rabbi Heschel and I would run into each other in the Seminary's cafeteria. If I saw him alone, I'd sit down beside him. If he saw me alone, he'd sit down beside me. In talking about the events of the day, we forged a common bond over the issue of civil rights, and through it a close personal relationship. He never called me Mrs. Fried. It was always Helenka. And in years to come, he would look to me to get a feeling of what was going on outside of the ivory tower of the Seminary.

I admired Rabbi Heschel greatly. To me, he was an outstanding human being. But, as I began to see, not everyone at the Seminary shared this feeling. At first there was talk along the order of, "Who is this guy coming in?"; "Will my course suffer because of him?" For a while, he was friendly with Dr. Saul Lieberman, the head of the Talmud department. Then they had a falling out. I never knew what caused the rift, but I somehow suspected Lieberman felt Heschel was getting too important.

He was important. He wrote prolifically and spoke throughout the country. He was one of the first to recognize and publicize the plight of Soviet Jewry. In the larger world, he was a very popular figure, but closer to home his fame and popularity were resented at times. He was not always accepted.

I wondered how I would be accepted when I was asked to attend the Midwest Branch Conference of Women's League in the spring of 1960, replacing the current president, Syd Rossman, who was ill. Until then the only conferences I had attended were along the Eastern seaboard. Though I was a vice president and being considered for the presidency, I was still an unknown quantity. And the Chicago group was made up of exceptional women.

But it turned out to be one of the most marvelous experiences I have ever had. The leadership in Chicago and I fit together so well. Blanche Lippitz in particular, an exacting person who had been president of Midwest Branch and was thoroughly involved in Judaism and Jewish affairs, was most positive about me and my speech. She was very confident in her opinions and somehow always right, so her reaction was quite important. The report that came back to National was glowing, and I do believe it contributed to my being nominated for the presidency.

Women's League had certainly become a major focus of my life. Still, the Marine Park Jewish Center and my friendships in the community remained very important, and I saw to it that Al Fried and I maintained our social life. One night we were having dinner with our friends and neighbors, Irwin and Lillian Winston. Irwin was an avid golfer and very fond of Al. For the longest time, Irwin had been urging him to visit the summer community in Copake, New York, a town in the foothills of the Berkshires, where he and Lillian had a home. This evening he really got into it. "Why are you still going to the Catskills?" he said. "Come up to Copake. The golf there is terrific, and the social life is great."

Afterwards Al said to me, "Let's go up and see what's doing there." So we did, and immediately we could see Irwin was right. It was a lovely lakefront community with houses instead of bungalows, a hotel, and a country club with an excellent golf course, swimming pool, and modern athletic facilities. Entertainment was provided by Broadway and television stars. And most importantly, there was a superior day camp and youth program for the children. The whole operation was way beyond what was available at a Catskill bungalow colony.

We decided to try it out. The first summer, we rented a place appropriately named the White House. It was very old, but I fixed it up so prettily with colorful curtains and some secondhand furniture. That summer was particularly hot, and luckily the White House was right on the lake. You'd walk out the back door, down a few steps, and you were in it. We spent the summer drifting in big tubes. The kids barely came up onto dry land.

Of course, we decided to go back. For the next few years, we rented the same house. Then we moved up to a nicer house on Oriole Road (all the roads in the development were named for birds) closer to the hotel.

The camaraderie, the entertainment, the facilities – all made the Copake community such an ideal summer place. And then there were the nearby cultural attractions in the Massachusetts part of the Berkshires. We went to the concerts at Tanglewood often and saw Leonard Bernstein conduct many a time. We also made lifelong friends. A good number were educators and officials of the Board of Education. Jay Green, chairman of the Board of Examiners, and his wife, Natalie, became our close friends. I often found myself playing against Natalie in a golf competition, but we were always good sports about it.

As would be expected, Al took to the golf course immediately, enrolling in the tournaments and winning many competitions. But when my friends first encouraged me to play, I said, "Count me out." I felt that I always had to do something productive and golf didn't seem productive enough. Until one day I tried it. Before long I was caught up and playing nearly every day. I was such a competitive person that once I got into it, I wanted to do my best, and so I joined the women's golf club and entered the tournaments.

The other women took lessons; I was too cheap to do that. The only lessons I ever took were from Al Fried. As a result, I never became an A player. But I was a high B player. Waiting to tee off, I never wasted time but worked on some creative and complicated piece of embroidery, and at the end of the summer I would have a really nice tablecloth or runner as well as a plaque or trophy for winning some competition.

Arthur and Michael had terrific summers up at Copake. Years later, Michael built his own home right beside the golf course. But when he was a kid, I could always count on Michael to get into some kind of mischief, and summers in Copake were no exception. When he was about twelve, I got a call from the camp director. Michael was one of four boys involved in starting a fire in part of the camp. Luckily they were able to put it out, but it could have been quite a terrible thing.

We mothers went down to an open area beside the lake to meet our kids when they returned from camp. The other women were saying they'd wait for their husbands to handle it.

The boys arrived. "I just heard something terrible," I said to Michael.

"Oh, it's not so bad, Mommy," he replied.

"What was it?"

"We were playing around and started a fire."

Without a moment's hesitation, I reared back and smacked his face so hard I thought his eyes would pop out of his head.

The other mothers were shocked. "How could you do that?" they said.

I felt it best to handle the situation at the moment.

As a rule, I didn't tell Al Fried about Michael's pranks. Among his more innocent ones were pulling the girls' long hair, although I always thought Michael viewed that gesture as a sign of affection.

One of the girls he liked was Lil Ruderman's daughter, Rhoda. The day after Michael's bar mitzvah, Al and I were having dinner at the Rudermans when the doorbell suddenly rang. Who walks in? Michael – dressed in the white tuxedo with colored cummerbund we had rented for his party the night before. He was determined to get his money's worth and, at the same time, make an impression on Rhoda – without pulling her hair.

After we had been going to Copake for a number of years, my friend Cynthia Kamen, who owned her summer home, called me one day and said, "You know, I'm sure the house behind me is going to be sold. A mother and daughter are living there, and the son-in-law is always fighting with the mother. It's not a good situation."

Sure enough, the house came up for sale. I hesitated because that was the year I was coming into the Women's League presidency, and I knew very well it wasn't going to be a white-glove presidency. The house had very little in the way of furnishings since the family hadn't lived there very long, and besides, I wouldn't have wanted their furniture anyway. I'd have to start from scratch. How could I find the time to furnish a house and prepare myself for the presidency? But Al was insistent that we buy the house then and there. And so we did. It cost $13,000 – which we thought was a lot of money. We put $7,000 down.

I immediately went into a whirlwind of activity, enlisting the help of my sister, Nettie, who had become a successful interior decorator by this time. There were windows all around the kitchen and dining room, and Nettie selected a fabric that was a wild print of turquoise, blues, and greens for the shades. I was a little dubious; it was so dramatic. But I went with her advice and reupholstered two armchairs that I brought up from the house in Brooklyn in solid lavender to anchor the shades. And then Al and I went around to antique shops and added some interesting pieces to the mix. It ended up looking just the way I wanted it to, not like a country house but a comfortable, yet sophisticated home. By the time the summer season began, it was all done.

After Al died, there were times I thought of selling the house, but I never did. And I am glad for that. It has turned out to be what I call a love house. Both our sons and my stepdaughter, Marsha, would spend part of their honeymoons there.

1962, to paraphrase Frank Sinatra, was a very good year. We bought the house in Copake. I became president of Women's League. And Al and I visited Israel for the first time.

In years to come, I would go to Israel more times than I can remember;

I stopped counting after my hundredth visit. Arthur and his family would move there, reason enough for many and many a visit. I would get to know a good number of very prominent Israelis, important figures in the government, philanthropies, and the arts. And I would have many extraordinary experiences in the nascent and growing Jewish state. But the trip of May 1962 holds a special place in my heart because it was the first.

Our tour was designed by United Synagogue and geared towards Conservative congregations, members of men's clubs and sisterhoods. At the last minute, the husband of Syd Rossman became ill, and she was unable to make the trip. It then fell to me, as incoming president of Women's League, to assume responsibility. Our group of 165 flew to Paris, traveled by train to Lucerne, and then continued on to Rome. From there we flew to Israel.

It was a very exciting time. Traveling abroad was not very common then, and Israel was still a new nation. We were kind of pioneers among the people we knew. Eva and Morris Ezra were joining us, and Isabel Josephsberg threw us a going away party where we received lovely gifts that we could use on our trip.

We were in the Air France terminal at JFK when there was an announcement that some mechanical problems had developed, and the departure would be delayed until the next day. Passengers would be put up around the airport overnight. We lived so close to the airport that I said to Al Fried, "Let's just go home."

But he was adamant. "Oh no," he said. "We're starting our vacation tonight."

It's a good thing we did because unbeknownst to us, Arthur and Michael had planned a party at the house that night. Had we shown up unexpectedly, we would have really messed it up for them.

In Paris we stayed at the Ambassador Hotel on the Boulevard Hausmann. I can still picture its bright red awnings, carpeting, and upholstery and the bouquet of bright red roses that awaited us, a gift from Al's cousins who lived in Paris.

A branch of Al's family had immigrated to France instead of the United States, and I had been in touch with one of the cousins, Francois Mandereux, a prominent lawyer and professor of law at the Sorbonne. He arranged for us to get together and meet the rest of the family. They were all very intellectual and accomplished and so happy to meet us – even though we arrived a day late, and they couldn't imagine what had happened to us.

It was such a shocking revelation for Al and me to learn what they had gone through during the war. Francois' sister, Ida, told us that early on during the Nazi occupation of Paris, her mother baked a meat loaf with her valuable jewelry inside, put the meat loaf in a picnic basket, and had Ida, who was just a little girl at the time, bring the basket over to the mother's best friend, who had promised to safeguard the jewelry until the end of the war.

Ida said she could still recall how frightened she felt walking down the streets with the basket until she reached the home of her mother's best friend, who took the basket, kept the jewelry, and denounced her mother to the Gestapo. The mother was deported. The rest of the family somehow managed to disperse and survive, but none of them ever saw their mother again.

They were such a wonderful family; being with them was so enlightening. Ida took me shopping in places unknown to the tourist trade. I bought the most exquisite hand-embroidered gloves and a beaded evening bag that seemed too expensive at the time but turned out to be well worth the price, for after all these years, I still use it.

Since I planned to buy a piece of original art in Israel, I limited my shopping in Europe and didn't accompany the women in our group when they went bargain hunting in the afternoon after a morning of sightseeing. But when they returned from their shopping sprees, I'd see what they bought, and if I thought something was really worthwhile, I'd go just to that specific place and buy just that item. In this way, I shopped quickly and carefully, getting perfume in Paris, linens in Lucerne, and leather goods in Rome. There were wonderful bargains to be had back then, when the dollar was so strong compared to the European currencies.

I was disappointed that United Synagogue had made no arrangements for us to see any of the synagogues in Europe. "We could be any kind of group instead of United Synagogue," I told Rabbi Hilsendrath, one of the three rabbis who accompanied us. "When we get to Lucerne, I think we should look up a synagogue and attend services."

As a result, we went to *Shabbat* services at a Lucerne synagogue that had a very contemporary feel even though it was Orthodox. Sitting upstairs, I spotted a very smart-looking woman, dressed in a beautifully tailored suit and fur hat. I walked over to her and introduced myself. When I told her what we were about, she was almost angry. "Why didn't you tell me you were going to be here in advance?" she said. "We would have done something in honor of your visit." Then she added, "I'll tell you what. Handpick a group of your people. Make sure none of them have a heart condition, because I want you to bring them to my house for *havdalah*, and they will have to go up a very steep hill."

This was Eva Wiener, who was to become a good friend. Later that afternoon a group of us arrived at Eva's magnificent contemporary house, which had been written up in the *House Beautiful* magazine of that region. Right next to the house was a similar looking building, which was actually the children's clothing factory owned by Eva's husband. Every doorway in both the house and factory had a built-in *mezuzah*.

Eva had an impressive art collection, but what fascinated me the most was a painting called *Hohekreisch*, the term for the naming ceremony of a baby girl. It was a custom peculiar to French, German, and Swiss Jews, where family and friends would stand over the cradle and sing three times, "What shall we name the baby?" Then they would sing the name: "Miriam, Miriam, Miriam," and dance around the cradle. The painting depicted just such a scene with gifts piled in the corner of the room. It was so evocative; you could feel the excitement. Years later Eva donated the painting to the Israel Museum in Jerusalem, where it hangs to this day.

In those years, we didn't make a fuss when a girl was born. But I thought the custom so beautiful that when I returned home, I suggested to some members of the National Board at Women's League that we inform our members about it and encourage naming ceremonies for baby girls. The first to respond to my suggestion was Adele Ginzberg, whose late husband was Louis Ginzberg, the famed Talmudist and Seminary professor. "Ugh!" she said, "that's ridiculous. We used to do that in Germany a long time ago. No one does it any more." She was against anything that seemed to be old fashioned. Nowadays naming ceremonies for baby girls is so common. Back then, "Mama Ginzberg" effectively squelched the idea.

In Rome we encountered dozens of vendors selling cameos. One of them was a nuisance until he took a good look at me and saw I was wearing a pin from *Torah* Fund with Hebrew lettering. "Oh, you're Jewish," he said – in Yiddish. "God bless you, God bless you. Where are you going?"

"To Israel," I told him.

"*Koif-nisht du* (don't buy here)," he said. "*Alla genaven* (all thieves). Spend your money in Israel."

The flight from Rome to Israel was so exciting because we were flying El Al. This was our plane. The attendants spoke Hebrew. We were coming home. When the plane landed in Israel, I felt an all-encompassing sensation; my life seemed complete. I had finally come to the land my grandfather had spoken of so often as if in a dream. When he said, "Next year in Jerusalem," I always believed he really meant it. Now I put my foot down on the soil and it was as if a powerful current of electricity shot through me. I didn't want to move.

On the bus en route from Lod Airport to Jerusalem, the tour leader pointed out the prison where Adolph Eichmann was being incarcerated. "A prison? A prison? It can't be," I said. I couldn't conceive of there being a prison in Israel. But I had no problem accepting the olive and eucalyptus trees along the road. We'd heard stories of how Israeli pioneers had made a land of milk and honey out of the desert, but to actually see the groves of citrus trees, the flowers, the fertile land bursting with produce was something else.

As the bus turned off the highway to enter Jerusalem, the rabbis on the tour asked Al Fried to recite the *Shehecheyanu* to express our joy and thankfulness for having lived to see this day, and he did it with all his heart.

I was so proud of him for that and also for the way he attended to three older women in our group who were traveling alone. All during the tour, Al Fried took it upon himself to help them with their baggage, to assist them in getting on and off the bus, to see they were comfortably seated in the restaurants. He treated them as if each were his own mother.

We stayed at the King David Hotel, already known all over the United States because of the movie *Exodus*. David Ben-Gurion was a guest there along with his wife, who I remember always carried a pocketbook with her wherever she went, just like Queen Elizabeth. With his crown of white hair, Ben-Gurion was such a familiar figure and immediately recognized by all. He was extremely friendly to our group.

It was a very, very busy tour. We got on the bus early in the morning and didn't get back to the hotel until nightfall. We visited Hebrew University, which was already a major educational institution, and I was so delighted and proud to discover that American medical students were working at

Hadassah Hospital – I was an active Hadassah member by this time. While in Haifa, we went to the Technion University and learned there was an exchange program between its students and the Massachusetts Institute of Technology – it was a school so much ahead of its time.

We were taken to the beautiful Baron Rothschild Gardens on Mount Carmel named for the Rothschild patriarch. He was called *Av Hayishuv*, Father of the Settlement, because he had given so much money towards a number of the early settlements in the mid-nineteenth century. "I want to be buried here on Mount Carmel," he had said, and in 1954 the Baron and his wife were reinterred on this site. At their *Yahrtzeit*, people from all the settlements he helped establish still come to this place of burial for a special commemoration.

Our tour brought us to the city of the mystics, Safed, which was already becoming a colony for Israeli artists. The evening we arrived, I said to Al Fried, "I want to buy some original art, but it will be very difficult to make a decision with a lot of people around me. Tomorrow, you go on the tour as planned without me. Tell the others I wasn't up to coming along."

The next morning I waited until the buses had left. Then I walked over to the hilly area where the galleries and studios were located. This was the oldest part of Safed, where the streets were cobbled stairways that turned into narrow byways and alleys. There were cats all over the place, sunning themselves on the stone walls, slinking in and out of passageways.

I explored different studios until I came to David Gilboa's gallery. His collection of impressionistic paintings of Israeli scenes appealed to me greatly. I selected one and asked him to put it aside. "I'll come back with my husband tonight," I told him. "And if he likes the painting, I'll buy it."

From there I stopped at another gallery that was totally empty. But no sooner did I begin looking around when a group of people assembled in front. I took a look; it was our group. "I'm going to have to hide," I said to the owner. "I don't want these people to see me."

He shoved me into a small room in the back. I couldn't see, but I could hear what was going on – above all Eva Ezra announcing in a loud voice, "*Tzeig mir. Ich hub gelt. Ich vill koifen.*" (Show me. I have money. I will buy.) As if to say, don't bother with the others. I'm the real thing. As much as I loved Eva, I was so ashamed of her. And I was sure whatever she liked, I wouldn't want to go near.

That night I told Al about the painting I had found. Together we walked back to the neighborhood with all the galleries and all the cats. But in the darkness, I couldn't tell one from the other. We climbed up and down the hilly streets until finally I saw one large, brightly lit studio that I remembered had paintings by all the artists. "Let's go in there. I'm sure they'll be able to tell us where the gallery we're looking for is located," I said.

The owner tried to direct us to David Gilboa's studio but it seemed so complicated. "Please take my hand and bring us over there," I pleaded. He did. Al loved the painting. We bought it, and I still have it hanging in my home.

This first trip to Israel was filled with thrills, not least among them being invited to the home of President Zalman Shazar. His wife was most charming and cordial. But at one point she said to me, "I can't imagine why American women's synagogue organizations don't hold their conventions here in Israel." Of course she didn't realize how difficult that was back in 1962.

Still, she planted a bug within me. I put her suggestion aside but I did not forget it. I knew I would not be able to act on it right away. But as soon as it was possible, I said to myself, this was something I was going to make happen.

VII

TRIUMPH AND TRAGEDY

Over the years, the Marine Park Sisterhood regularly scheduled weekends at the Concord Hotel in the Catskills. Since I made the arrangements, I got to know the owners, Mr. and Mrs. Winarick, very well. They were wonderful hosts, always generous to us. Now that I was about to be installed as president of Women's League, I thought the Concord would be the ideal site for our November 1962 convention.

There was no hotel in the greater New York area that offered more in terms of sports facilities and entertainment than the Concord. But the very wealth of activities, which always made it so desirable for sisterhood weekends, proved to be somewhat of a distraction to the delegates at our agenda-packed convention. What with its "Monster" golf course, and the fact that it snowed towards the end of the convention and the women from places like Florida and California had to be restrained from running out of doors to make snowmen and throw snowballs, the Concord was almost too much of a good thing. But truly it was one of the great Catskill resorts, and a natural site for Women's League conventions. Because the Winaricks were so hospitable to us and gave us so many extras, we always ended up making money on the conventions. That was most unusual. Generally the best you can hope for is to break even.

Our membership in 1962 was about 200,000. Fifteen hundred delegates from throughout the United States and Canada descended on the Concord. Many of the husbands came as well. As I was being installed as president, not only was Al Fried there, but my mother and Arthur with his fiancée, Susan Braverman. Even Michael, who was a student at Michigan State then, came in for the event.

Before going down to the Imperial Room, the Concord's enormous nightclub, where the installation was to take place, I threw a little party in our suite for the other incoming officers. Somehow, walking across the room, Michael caught the leg of his pants on the edge of a chair, and the entire seam, from top to bottom, split. He looked down dismally at his ripped trousers; it was the only pair he had with him. "I just won't go," Michael cried.

"Just a minute," I said, calming him down. This was before the days when sewing kits were provided in every hotel room. But as a long-time sewer, I never traveled without needle and thread. Michael went into an adjoining room, took off his pants and gave them to me. I turned them inside out, sewed the seam, and all was well.

My installation was one of the outstanding events of my life. Never did I dream when I joined Mama's Ladies' Auxiliary of the Marine Park Jewish Center and first discovered there was such a thing as Women's League, that I would become its president. I knew it would take four years out of my life. My leadership courses would have to be put on hold. I wouldn't have time for golf. But I would be in a position to make significant contributions to American Jewish life.

All through the convention, I felt the presence of my grandfather, Isaac Boehm. After all, it was in his home that I first became exposed to the Conservative movement. What would he think if he knew his granddaughter was the head of the organization representing Conservative women from all over North America?

Afterwards I thought of my grandfather often, as I moved through the halls of the Seminary, sat through many a meeting, and struggled with the range of issues with which I was confronted as president. How would he handle a particular situation, I would ask myself. There were quite a few contentious issues. My efforts to get Women's League to take a stand on civil rights met with some success, but I was frustrated in attempts to get a resolution passed opposing the Vietnam War. The Conservative movement as a whole did not want to express a viewpoint on this issue, and we could not go out on our own.

In 1964 I was sworn in for my second term of office, this time in Chicago. Up to then, most of the conventions had been held on the East Coast.

We felt it was time for us to reach out nationally, and the women in Chicago were confident they would be able to accommodate all our needs.

But somehow, their best laid plans went astray. For one thing, it was snowing most of the time, making it difficult for us to get around. For another, unlike the Concord, the hotel was not up to the demands of the event. There were problems with the elevators and worse, with the food. Although we never pinpointed the exact cause, something was served that caused a widespread stomach ailment. The hotel's pharmacist said that in all his years, he never had such a run on Pepto Bismol. And yet the program was one of the best ever. Mim Teplitz and I worked very hard to create it; many others were involved. What a pity that so well-planned and well-attended a convention was not as successful as we had hoped.

During those tumultuous days, I was reminded of Mrs. Zalman Shazar. The seeds of the idea she planted within me had lain dormant for two years. Now they began to sprout.

I brought my idea to the board. We would not adjourn this problem-riddled convention but would reconvene the following year – in Jerusalem.

Although most took to it immediately, others were doubtful. "How can you think of Israel?" some said. "It will be too complicated to plan a convention there. It's too far away. Many of the women have never even been to Israel."

"Well," I said, "this is the chance for them to go."

At our final session, I concluded my address with the words: "Next year in Jerusalem!" And fifteen hundred women resoundingly echoed, "Next year in Jerusalem!" and burst into applause. It was very dramatic, very thrilling.

When we returned to New York from Chicago, we began planning. The reconvening would take place six months later, in May 1965. It was to be a two-week trip that would include flights, tours, and accommodations. We would tour the country for about a week and arrive at the King David Hotel in Jerusalem on the second Thursday. That would leave us the weekend to see Jerusalem before convening the convention, which would run from Sunday night through Tuesday.

The writer Rabbi Chaim Potok agreed to be our spiritual leader. But then he thought better of leaving his wife, who was in the final months of her pregnancy. Instead we invited Rabbi Max Wall from Burlington,

Vermont. There was a large sisterhood in Burlington, and Rabbi Wall was very much admired by the women in his community, and he turned out to be an excellent choice. He conducted services for our group, performed benedictions, and advised us on all spiritually-related matters.

One hundred and fifty delegates attended, many of whom had never been to Israel before. Quite a number of husbands accompanied their wives. Al was there for the whole thing. Morris came along with Eva. But Nathan, having not yet conquered his fear of flying, did not accompany Charlotte.

While still in America, I got a phone call from Teddy Kollek, the new mayor of Jerusalem. He begged me to release the rooms that we had at the King David Hotel for the days preceding the convention. The Israel Museum was being inaugurated just at that time. Many important figures were planning to attend, and there was a shortage of rooms at the better hotels.

We tried to find alternative space, but there was none to be had. This was a major problem. On the one hand, how could we turn down Mayor Kollek's request? The Israel Museum was a major institution; it was going to put Israel on the map as a dominant player in the world of art. Its opening was a matter of great priority. On the other hand, this convention was so significant to our organization. We had worked so hard to make it a success. What would we do for those days in Jerusalem?

Then we found out about a *kibbutz*, Kiryat Anavim, located in the Judean Hills west of Jerusalem. It was a secular *kibbutz* with a liberal atmosphere that was so right for our group. This would be the solution to our problem. I recruited some of the more active members of Women's League who ordinarily would be very put out by such a situation, who would cry, "Why should they do this to us? Why should we give up our rooms?" and I put them on a committee.

"Your role is to communicate with all the delegates and convince them what a wonderful experience it will be to stay at this *kibbutz*," I told them. Charlotte Levine headed the committee, and, as expected, she was most persuasive.

Then I appointed a committee to arrange for entertainment while we were there because I didn't want the women to be getting into taxis and going all over the place, especially on *Shabbat*. We wanted to keep them all on the farm, so to speak. This committee arranged for a concert one evening, a dance group another night, and a lecture still another night. And as things turned out, what seemed like such a terrible obstacle to the success of our trip became one of its highlights.

All of us had comfortable private rooms. We enjoyed the most delicious food. When we got to bed our first night in Kiryat Anavim, we sank into bed linens of the deepest down. It was chilly out of doors, and we had such a delightful night's sleep.

The dance group was great. They not only entertained us, they engaged us by teaching us Israeli folk dancing. The committee found Murray Greenfield, an art dealer and early *oleh* from New York, who installed an exhibition of paintings for us in the *kibbutz*. What with viewing the paintings and listening to Murray's lecture on the status and direction of Israeli art, our *Shabbat* afternoon was well spent.

On Sunday we moved on to the King David Hotel, where we met Billy Rose, the Broadway impresario, who had donated his important collection of sculptures to the Israel Museum. Later on I heard that David Ben-Gurion had asked Billy Rose whether he wasn't concerned about sending such valuable art to so dangerous a place as Jerusalem. "If you have any problems, you can melt them down and use them as bullets," the showman nonchalantly replied.

At the moment we met him, however, Billy Rose was anything but nonchalant. Some bureaucratic snafu had caused the delivery of his collection to be held up, and he was furious. Sitting near us in the coffee shop, he gestured to our table and said, "If these women had handled it, I'm sure the sculptures would have arrived with no problem."

In appreciation for our giving up the rooms, the director of the King David Hotel arranged for us to have the premier group tour of the Israel Museum. How impressed we were with this world-class museum. Israel was still such a new nation, only seventeen years old. Yet already it boasted a cultural institution of such international caliber.

President Shazar delivered the opening address of our convention. Professor Moshe Davis, who headed the Institute of Contemporary Judaism at Hebrew University, spoke to us about spiritual aspects of Israeli life. Dr. Zerah Warhaftig, the Israeli Minister of Religion, told us what high regard he had for our women and for our organization's accomplishments in the United States. "Women are the true leaders of Judaism," he declared. As I listened to him, I thought back to a conversation I'd had with Rabbi Wolfe

Kelman, Executive Director of the Rabbinical Assembly, a few months earlier. When he learned I planned to invite Dr. Warhaftig to speak at our convention, he said, "Forget it, Helen. He'll never come. He's Orthodox; he doesn't consider women religiously at all."

I had always counted on Rabbi Kelman for advice. But not this time. I invited Dr. Warhaftig anyway. And he came! And he spoke! And he was outstanding!

The culminating event of the convention was the presentation of the first Mathilde Schechter Award to Golda Meir, who was then Minister of Foreign Affairs. Before I became involved with Women's League, I had never heard of Mathilde Schechter. But as my involvement grew, I developed a great appreciation for what she accomplished and agreed it was high time to honor her name and memory with an award.

Before I presented her with this new Women's League award, I had never met Golda Meir. But I had heard much about the woman Ben-Gurion called the only real man in the *Knesset* and was so proud to share a podium with her. She was very serious, totally unfashionable, and marvelous. The only thing I couldn't stand about her was her chain smoking.

In her speech Golda Meir, who was born in Kiev and grew up in Milwaukee, made a plea for *aliyah*. She said Israel needs not only those who have to come to Israel, but those who want to come to Israel; not only the persecuted, but those who desire to be part of the Jewish State.

At that time, the entire religious establishment in Israel was totally controlled by the Orthodox. There were no more than half a dozen Conservative synagogues in the country, and none of them had sisterhoods. But the members of those congregations, both men and women, were delighted with our presence and attended our sessions. In addition we drew people from the larger secular population. People were very curious to learn what we were about.

Our presence was a shot in the arm for the Conservative movement in Israel, which until then had been small and unrecognized. We were written up in many of the newspapers and discussed in the media.

Years before, it was our sisterhood that became the impetus for the Marine Park Jewish Center to become an important synagogue in Brooklyn. Now it was the Women's League of the United States, Canada, and Mexico that helped project the Conservative movement into Israel's public consciousness. For the second time in my life, I found myself at the head of a women's organization that became a spearhead for a larger cause.

The convention in Jerusalem was among the more thrilling events of my presidency, but attending two White House conferences ranks up there as well. I will never forget when an invitation in a big envelope, addressed in beautiful calligraphy arrived. It was to a historic conference on civil rights entitled "To Serve These Needs" to be held on the lawn of the White House. Hundreds of people attended. President Johnson and Lady Bird spoke to us. Mrs. Johnson was particularly warm and gracious. I was wearing a hat as usual; she commented on it and engaged me in conversation. Who was I and what group did I represent, she wanted to know.

It was at this conference that I first heard the term "Affirmative Action." There was some discussion on the subject. Then a tall, very handsome black woman got up. I thought she would speak in favor of this new policy. But no, what she said was, "We don't want Affirmative Action. We just want equality. We want to be as equal as anyone else." She sat down and the group fell silent. I never found out who she was.

I was about to attend the White House conference on education when I broke my toe. Al Fried said, "Buy yourself a pair of shoes two sizes larger, tape up your toe, and go." But I was too cheap to buy a pair of shoes I couldn't wear afterwards, so I borrowed a pair from Natalie Green. There I was, the lady accustomed to dancing into a room on high heels, schlepping in with Natalie Green's big, flat shoes. But I still wore a hat.

Arthur Goldberg, who was a Supreme Court justice at that time, had been on the Seminary board; we knew each other casually. Now I spotted him standing alone at the edge of the temporary fence that separated the vips from the delegates. I approached him and we chatted for a while. "What's happening?" I asked. "I hear you may be stepping down from the Supreme Court."

"You'll be hearing all about it from the President," he said with a little smile. But I thought he seemed less than happy.

A while later President Johnson appeared and announced to the group that Arthur Goldberg would be resigning from the Supreme Court in order to become our ambassador to the United Nations. How exciting it was to hear such groundbreaking news firsthand.

During my presidency we broke ground for the Mathilde Schechter

Residence Hall on a grassy knoll right in the middle of the Seminary campus. Women's League had raised the funds for this greatly needed building for female students, and we were all most enthusiastic about it.

The ceremony took place on a beautiful summery day. Chancellor Louis Finkelstein, Attorney General Louis Lefkowitz, and Governor Nelson Rockefeller were among the many dignitaries who were present.

I had just concluded my remarks when Governor Rockefeller stepped up to the podium and stood beside me, looking out at the audience. "That was a wonderful speech," he said. "When you're finished with your presidency, look me up. I'll find some good position for you in my office." And as he spoke, he dropped his hand behind me and stroked my backside. I was so astonished that for the moment all I could think of was that Rabbi Finkelstein might have witnessed this inappropriate gesture. Moving quickly away, I thought to myself the Governor's reputation as a womanizer must be well deserved.

While I did not allow Rockefeller's behavior to spoil this wonderful day, as things turned out, the groundbreaking ceremony need not have been held at all. The Seminary board subsequently reversed itself and decided not to build the hall on the planned site. We had to search around for another one and finally settled on an off-campus locale.

I was outgoing president in November 1966 when our convention convened back at the Concord Hotel. This time, all went well. Elie Wiesel was our guest speaker. Before the convention, Rabbi Kelman forewarned me: "Mr. Wiesel is very shy and doesn't like to speak to many people. So you must take care of him by yourself."

Ruth Sussman, the daughter of my mentor, Helen Sussman, had agreed to pick Elie Wiesel up, drive him to the Concord, and take him back. By chance, we met in the elevator. My first impression was of a very, very timid man. All he could talk about was how he had to leave immediately after his speech. I assured him his ride was arranged; everything would be taken care of. Then I told him to go to his room and relax, and in a little while, someone would come to escort him down to the Imperial Room.

Before long, there was a tapping on my door. It was Elie Wiesel. "I don't know what to do," he said. "Some people have asked me to go down with them and have my photograph taken. Shall I go?"

"I wish you would," I said.

"Will you come with me?"

I could see I was his mommy so I said, "Yes, I'll come along."

After the picture taking, where he appeared most uncomfortable, we proceeded to an anteroom and were asked to sit in positions that corresponded to our places on the dais in the Imperial Room. My place was on one side and his was in the center.

"Am I the only man here?" he asked me.

"Oh, no," I told him. "Rabbi Teplitz will be here as well."

The next thing I know is we are all marching up towards the dais, and Elie Wiesel is right next to me. He had taken his name off his chair in the anteroom and exchanged it with the woman who was supposed to be sitting beside me. Up on the dais, Helen Sussman saw what happened and swiftly rearranged the order.

Now that we were seated beside each other, I tried to loosen him up a bit. I pointed out my family at a table right up front. I told him about Women's League and what we were doing. But nothing I said seemed to calm him down.

Finally Elie Wiesel was introduced. He proceeded to the podium and stood there silently. For some reason, he could not begin. I went over to him. "What's the matter?" I asked. "Do you need more light?"

"Maybe," he said.

We raised the lights a bit, and he began, very slowly at first. But then he picked it up. His speech was based on his recently released book, *The Jews of Silence*, which dealt with Jews living in the Soviet Union. People were not very aware of this subject in 1966. There was just the beginning of the recognition of the plight of Russian Jews, and it was Elie Wiesel who was responsible in large measure for bringing it to public attention. In his speech, he chided the women for not being involved enough in this cause.

"Now the Jews of Russia are alone in a world of evil, but they are not succumbing to it," he said. "They are afraid we are. They worry about us and pray for our future welfare. If we do not help ourselves to attain a more meaningful Jewish life, we will need their pity, their help."

To hear such strong words from one who appeared so frail was overwhelming, and the delegates were shaken. Some were offended by his outspokenness; they did not appreciate what sounded like a rebuke. But others, myself included, were most approving. I had had many discussions with Rabbi Heschel about the situation of Russia's Jews and thought Elie

Wiesel was performing a great *mitzvah* in bringing it to the attention of the American public.

After the speech was over, Ruth Sussman appeared, ready to take him home immediately as he had requested. But now that the speaking part was done and he was seated at a table and signing books, he was in his element and in no apparent hurry. Ruth was kept waiting for quite a while.

It had been my hope that Mim Teplitz would follow me as president of Women's League. She was one of the most important vice presidents, very talented and very well liked. She wrote and produced many of the important scripts we used for our conventions. But Mim was married to Saul Teplitz, rabbi of Congregation Sons of Israel in Woodmere, and there was an unwritten policy that the wife of a rabbi should not be considered for the presidency of Women's League.

I think Mim was a little bitter over not being nominated, but I also think it pushed her to prepare for a professional life. She became an outstanding social worker. Years later, when my mother came back from Florida and was living with me, Mim helped me a great deal through a difficult time. Being the wife of the rabbi of a prominent synagogue in Woodmere may have given her a certain edge, but she was most accomplished and successful in her work.

Towards the end of my presidency I was representing Women's League at a meeting of the Jewish Braille Institute in their building on East Seventy-fourth Street, a private residence that had been converted into office space. Now I overheard some discussion about plans to sell the property. We at Women's League were operating out of a small office in the Seminary. Our organization had grown in scope and size. It was time we had a home of our own. I came back to Women's League and told everyone what a good opportunity it would be to buy this building.

Evelyn Henkind, an exceptional Women's League leader who would follow me as president, wouldn't hear of it. She didn't want to think of undertaking such a move. I wouldn't let go of the idea, however, and finally convinced a number of the women on the Executive Committee to look into it. They did. It took a while, but we bought the building, and a few years later we moved in. Many years after that, when the building needed major renovations and was no longer the right space for us, we sold it at a handsome profit. But for the more than thirty years it was home to Women's League, it served us very well.

I would have to say to this point in time I had led a rather charmed life. Of course, it was terrible when my father died. I loved him dearly, and it was such a sudden, unexpected death. Still, to lose a parent is part of the natural order of things. But then, early in 1967, Al Fried went into New York Hospital for a routine operation, and things took a terrible turn.

At first we thought nothing of it. "Just polyps," Dr. Globus said. "He'll be home soon." Shortly afterwards, however, Al began to feel quite sick once again. He had always been so robust and healthy that I couldn't imagine it could be anything serious. I was waiting in the hospital while he underwent the second surgery. Arthur and Michael had just walked down the hall when the doctor came over to me. "Mrs. Fried, I'm terribly sorry but the news is not good," he said. I cut him off. "I don't want my kids to know. Let's just say all went well."

Seeing the doctor, Arthur and Michael approached us and heard me say, "I'm so glad it was so successful. Thank you very, very much."

They went off happily while the doctor gave me the details. The cancer was in the stomach and colon and had already invaded the liver.

"How long does he have to live?" I asked.

"It will be within the year."

That night I went home to an empty house with a heavy heart. Arthur was married already. Michael was out with some friends. My mother was away in Florida. All alone, I tried to digest the news. I couldn't believe it. I was such an optimist that I held out the hope they would find some way to treat the cancer. Then, I thought, of all places it had gone to the liver.

They gave Al some kind of chemotherapy. But it didn't help. Still, I never told him what was really wrong with him. To the kids I said, "Dad's fine. They took the cancer out, and it didn't spread."

I covered up with my sons, the rest of the family, Al's clients. For his part, Al wouldn't give in. After his surgery healed, he forced himself to get dressed and go to work. He would schlep himself, really, really schlep himself on the bus, on the subway, coming home very tired. He went to work as long as he could. He didn't want anyone to know. But by the late spring it got so bad, we had to tell people. It was wretched, absolutely wretched.

Summer came, and I thought Al would be better off in Copake. He had loved it there from the start. We hired an ambulance to bring him up.

The day after we arrived, Rabbi Heschel called. "Helenka," he said, "you have got to come back to New York to march with Martin Luther King. We will hold hands and march together."

"Rabbi," I said, "if Al were better, there is nothing I would love to do more. But we just got him up here, and I can't leave him."

"Helenka, you are right. You can't leave him, and you shouldn't leave him. You are where you belong. I will be thinking about both of you."

Al was dying, and I knew I would have to go to work if I wanted to continue living in the style I was used to. We had a house with a mortgage. We had a summer house with a mortgage. We had a car. We lived a nice full life that I could never continue with just my volunteer work and teaching a course to a group of women here and there.

Before we came up to Copake, I went down to the employment office at New York University, where I was interviewed by a young student named Dennis Weintraub. "I'll get you a job," he said. And he did, at the Brooklyn College of Pharmacy at Long Island University. I would teach two courses, six hours a week in their commercial department.

After we were up in Copake for a week, Dennis Weintraub suddenly called. "Mrs. Fried, I've got something wonderful for you. A full-time teaching slot in the City University of New York."

"Great," I said. "Which school?"

"Manhattan Community College."

I took a deep breath. Michael, who had just graduated from college, was teaching psychology and working in the financial aid office at Manhattan Community.

"I don't know," I said to Dennis. "My son is there. I don't want to move into his territory."

"Look," he said, "I sewed up this job for you. All you have to do is go down for an interview with Dr. Connolly, the chairman of the speech department. I won't send anyone else there because I know they will go for you."

"Let me get back to you."

I called Michael and told him I had an opportunity to teach full time. It was just what I needed; the income would be good.

"That's wonderful," he said.

"Michael, do you know a Dr. Connolly?"

"Oh no, don't tell me it's at my school."

"Look, Michael," I said, "you think about it. And if you have any reservations about my working in that school, just say so. I'll understand."

There was some silence on the phone. Then he said, "Mother, how can I stand in your way? I know how important it is to you. But I don't want anyone in the school to know you are my mother." It sounded like I was a disease.

My next problem was, how do I leave Al Fried to go down to New York for the interview? But I had a wonderful coterie of friends. They all said, "Don't worry. We'll take care."

Early the next morning, I got on the train. My interview went very well. They looked over my record and even though I had no experience in higher education, I was hired. Dennis had convinced the people at Manhattan Community College that I would be right for the job. How, I don't know.

Meanwhile Al's condition got much worse. We brought him back to Brooklyn. "Mrs. Fried," the doctor said to me, "it will be very difficult for me to get your husband back into the hospital, but it will be even more difficult for him and for you if he remains at home. I'll get him back on a pretext. We can do another little operation to justify his admission and keep him in the hospital for the last part of his life."

What happened was that Al would fill up with a lot of muck, and they used a machine to suction it from his body so he could go on breathing. The machine kept him alive longer. As I think about it now, I wonder whether that was the right thing to do. But at the time, it seemed so.

Al was aware and alert until close to the end. He didn't want to see anybody but the family. I passed the word along. But Sol Henkind, a friend who was good company, always telling funny stories, wouldn't listen to me. I'm glad he didn't, because he was able to make Al Fried laugh.

I began teaching that fall. The college was in an office building in the 50s, near Sixth Avenue. I would visit Al in the hospital on the Upper East Side, then get in the car and drive over to the college.

There I would open the door to the classroom with a very heavy heart and tears in my eyes, and suddenly I would turn into a different person. My husband was dying? My family was terribly unhappy? That was another life. Here I was in charge. I was teaching.

What was wrong with me, I wondered. I must be the biggest fake in the world. How could I walk into that classroom prepared to teach, do a good job, and then go back to my dying husband? I had a great deal of conflict over that.

But teaching was my saving grace. What it taught me was, if you're troubled, do something for someone else, and you will be doing something for your own self – yes, for your own health and survival. And I was doing a good job for those students. I was reaching them.

Throughout the whole ordeal, my boys were so wonderful. At first they didn't know how grave the situation was. But as time moved on, they understood. After Arthur and Susan's first baby, Alissa Rachel, was a few weeks old, they brought her to the house. Al was in bed. We brought the baby up to the bedroom and lay her down beside him. And the peaceful look it brought to Al's face never left me. It reminded me of the time Al's mother was dying. Arthur was a baby then, and we lay him down beside her in the same way. It was so strange. In both cases, we witnessed one life going out and another life coming in.

Whenever possible, Michael would drive me around during these terrible days. I had been driving for so long, but I never really enjoyed it, and it was a relief to be driven from one place to another. But one Friday afternoon towards the end, I visited Al and then drove home alone.

I opened the door and there was Michael, waiting for me. He had prepared a hot meal, a typical *Shabbat* meal of chicken soup and chicken. I lit the candles and the two of us had dinner together. Bringing the spoon of hot soup mixed with bitter tears to my lips, I looked across the table at my handsome son. What a handful he had been at times, so willful, so wont to childhood pranks and mischief. Now here he was, a young man, filled with the anguish of his father's impending death, and in his grief reaching out to make things easier for his mother.

The next day I told Al Fried about it. "Helen," he said, "I always told you in our old age we're going to get a lot of *naches* from Michael."

Al Fried had said to Rabbi Besdin, "Give me something I can read."

"Just do the *Shema*," the rabbi said. That is the prayer that affirms faith in one God: "Hear, Oh Israel, the Lord our God, the Lord is One."

We kept a *siddur* on the table beside Al's bed, and I pinched down the page with the *Shema*. Whenever I visited Al, I would read it in English and Hebrew. The day he died, I read it to him. Unbeknownst to me, Arthur had been there that day and read it to him. So had Michael.

From start to finish, I said to myself as long as Al's not suffering and I'm taking care of him, I have to be satisfied with what I have. God had been good to me all these years, and I had faith that everything would fall into place. Even Al's death would fall into place. And it did. He died that December. I had gotten a college teaching job, and a new life began.

But Al Fried was the first love of my life. I never forgot that. I never forgot how much I loved him nor how proud I was to have married the man who wouldn't deign to look at the chubby little girl who adored him when he was the handsome high school senior.

PART THREE

VIII

MOVING ON

I GOT UP FROM SITTING *SHIVA* and tried to pull myself together. I said to myself, Al isn't going to be around for me any more. I have to move forward.

But it was very difficult.

We got Mother off to Florida. She mourned Al greatly; she had loved him like a son. But her life would go on just the same. Mine was ripped apart.

The grief was wrenching. I no longer had Al to talk to, to cuddle up to and sleep with, to even express the pain I now was feeling. When I was teaching or otherwise occupied out of the house, the pain was bearable. But at home I felt very bereft. I would look over to the other side of the bed, to the empty pillow beside me and cry myself to sleep.

But you know what? I don't remember how long it took, at the time it felt much too long, but gradually, very gradually, I was able to look over to the other side of the bed, and isn't it strange? I didn't miss him as much as I had. Life goes on. You never forget. But the pain, the hurt of the loss of someone so dear to you fades into the background.

When I came back to school after the *shiva*, I walked into the room, took a look at the students sitting there expectantly, and impulsively I told them how helpful teaching them had been to me at a time when I was so pained. Oddly this was one of the few speeches I have given in my life that was impromptu. It moved along with such ease because it was so deeply felt. And I could see from the expressions on their faces how deeply I was reaching them. It was a living lesson for them, and towards the end of the semester, we discussed it and evaluated it as a speech of appreciation.

I was so fortunate to have gotten this job at Manhattan Community College and so thankful to Dennis Weintraub for getting it for me. I had a lot of learning to do, for once again I was thrown into a position for which I was really not prepared. And at first, I wondered whether I would be able to live up to the job.

Although by then I had been a practicing public speaker for years, in terms of professional training, I didn't feel qualified to teach the subject. After all, I had taken only one speech course as an undergraduate. Like the time I taught typing at the Rhodes School, I had to teach myself how to teach others. I read as much as I could, worked as hard as I could, and tried to do something innovative every day. And from the way my students reacted to me, I sensed everything was going to be fine. I watched them listening; I could see they were receiving my message. Teaching became my solace.

So did the love and support of my sons. They were there for me not only through the dark time of Al's illness but the difficult year that followed his death. Both said *kaddish* for the eleven months following a parent's death, and Arthur, much like his father, became more devoted to the religious life during that period. He got into the habit of going to the Brooklyn Jewish Center regularly on *Shabbat*. Rabbi Israel Levanthal hoped he would take a leading role, perhaps even become president. Arthur couldn't because his work took up so much of his time. Nevertheless, he was very serious about his attendance.

He regularly sat beside a young man, the son of a rabbi. Around them, the men would talk about the stock market or their golf game. The women could sit with the men, but they often congregated in the back row. When the conversations became too loud, the principals on the *bimah* would admonish the women to quiet down, when, in truth, the men were making equally as much noise.

One day the young man said to Arthur, "You know, there's an Orthodox synagogue nearby on St. John's Street that meets earlier in the morning. Let's try it out."

The synagogue was small, not nearly as grand as the Brooklyn Jewish Center. But prayer there was essential, and distractions were minimal. They also had a study group in the afternoon that Arthur enjoyed very much. Before long, not only had Arthur switched to this little *shul*, he was generously supporting it. He still does. And as a result of his affiliation, he became more observant.

Arthur had met Susan at the Marine Park Jewish Center when they were both in high school. He was in charge of the synagogue cloak room when there were special events, and I always said that after all the coats were hung up, they closed the door and got to know each other.

Susan was a superior student and a fantastic kid all around, good in sports, talented in music. I liked her right away, although I wished she would do more for herself. She never cared about dressing. What was going on in her soul was important, not how she looked. But as a bride, dressed in a lovely gown and wearing a little makeup, she was absolutely beautiful.

I was very careful what I said to her. Later on I would buy something I thought would look good on her and tell her I bought it for myself. "I can't use it, but I can't return it either, Susan," I'd say. "Why don't you try it on?" Most of the time, she would take it from me.

Her mother was a fashion plate. Maybe Susan was rebelling against that. Certainly she did the opposite of her mother in having seven children, while she was an only child.

Arthur and Susan were married at the Union Temple on Eastern Parkway. The ceremony was most unusual, as it was performed by three rabbis representing the three streams of American Judaism at that time: the Reform Rabbi Stanley Dreyfus of Union Temple, the Orthodox Rabbi Abraham Besdin who had bar mitzvahed Arthur, and the Conservative Rabbi Saul Teplitz, our dear friend.

Neither Arthur nor Susan wanted to go away to college because they didn't want to separate. Consequently, both got their excellent educations locally – Arthur at Baruch and Susan at Brooklyn College. But when it was time for Michael to go to college, he was ready to go away from home and enrolled at Michigan State.

While Michael was there, I would make every effort to get speaking assignments from the Seminary or Women's League in the Lansing vicinity. In that way, I got to visit him several times a year. He had bought himself a used Plymouth Barracuda, the same shade of green as the car we had when he was a little boy. Still a Mr. Fix-it, Michael could take the car apart, repair it, and put it together again. He fixed the front seat so that it would go all the way back, making it an ideal car for necking.

He was a good-looking kid, very popular – and not only because of his car. The Passover of his last term at college he couldn't come home. So he made *Pesach* at Michigan State for all the other Jewish kids who couldn't come home, using recipes that he had learned while helping me. The main course was chicken, which he had cut up and marinated in salad dressing overnight and then baked with *matzoh* meal. He got a bunch of *Haggadot* and conducted a regular *seder*. It seemed to me Michael had turned out to be very much like me in that he could handle anything, do anything. And if it didn't turn out right, he would say it will be better the next time.

He had an apartment that at first he shared with a couple of boys and then kept on his own. Every time I visited, he had a slew of the most adorable, but not Jewish, girls running after him. "I don't understand you," I'd say to him. "You come from such a Jewish family. How could you be going around with these *shiksas*?"

"Oh Mom," he'd say, "the Jewish girls around here are all dogs."

Once I told him, "I have a friend who lives around here. I'm sure her daughter isn't a dog. Come with me and I'll introduce you to her."

He said, "You go first and see what she's like."

I did. She was okay, maybe not as sexy as the other girls he was seeing. He looked her up, but he never dated her.

The last time I saw Michael at Michigan State, I noticed a girl's belongings lying around. "What's this nightgown doing here?" I asked.

And he said, "Oh you know how it is, Mother. Sometimes the girls stay over."

But it wasn't girls, it was one girl. Her name was Nancy, and I had a suspicion Michael and Nancy were very cozy with each other.

Michael had always said to me, "Mom, I won't marry anyone but a Jewish girl, believe me."

And I did for a long time, until after he graduated and had returned home. One day, I emptied the pockets of a jacket of his before bringing it to the cleaners and found a rent receipt from an apartment on Ocean Avenue.

"What is this, Michael?"

"Oh, I just helped Nancy out with her rent," he said to me, sloughing it off.

She was here.

On her birthday, he brought her to the house. Al Fried was seriously ill then and in bed. He walked down the stairs in his bathrobe. I introduced them, and he was very pleasant. But afterwards he said to me, "I will never accept her. I will have nothing to do with her." And to Michael, he later said, "If you have any intention of marrying this girl, I want you to know right now you will no longer be welcome in this house."

I just could not accept that approach.

One day at the Seminary, I ran into Rabbi Henry Michaelman. "Oh, Helen, I'm converting your future daughter-in-law," he said to me. Wow, I could have gone through the floor. I had no idea it had gone so far. "And I want to tell you, she's not a very stable girl." That was some combination.

Soon after, I was straightening out Michael's room when the telephone rang. It was Nancy. I lingered because I wanted to know what was going on. From what I could gather, she was at the *mikveh* and wanted him to come down there. And he said to her, "Remember, you are not doing this for me. You are doing it because this is the kind of life you want to lead."

When he hung up the phone, I laced into him. "You are terrible. She is doing this for you, and you should be there with her." But he was very firm; he would not go.

He said to me, "Look, Mother, I've heard you say that a convert must be treated even nicer than someone born Jewish, because he or she chose it."

I knew where this came from. The previous January, Michael was with me when I was the Friday night guest speaker at a synagogue in Baltimore. Al Fried and I had planned to drive down together, stay for the weekend, make a little trip out of it. But he was already not feeling well and Michael, who was home from college for intersession then, had agreed to come in his place.

The topic was intermarriage. Michael had taken what I said to heart and remembered it well. What could I say now? Nevertheless, I didn't feel right about it, and the reason I didn't feel right about it was because I knew Al Fried would not accept Nancy. How could I lay such a thing on him?

It was such a difficult time. My husband was dying; my son was about to marry a convert. It was one of the roughest periods of my life.

Then Nancy brought Michael to her home. She came from a small town outside of Lansing, where her mother was very active in her community and had just married the town banker. Her mother said to Nancy, "You know Michael is a very nice boy and I don't object to your marrying him. But I don't want anyone in this town to know he is Jewish."

Foolishly, Nancy told Michael. It floored him, and he broke up with her. Afterwards Nancy came back to New York and tried to recapture the relationship. But it was over for him.

The school year began. Michael met an attractive brunette at Manhattan Community, and he and Janet began dating regularly. They would hang around in his room for hours. My mother would say to me, "What are they doing upstairs all this time?"

"Mother," I'd reply, "what do you think a young man and woman would be doing?"

One day in the spring, Janet came downstairs. "Michael and I want to get married," she said, "and I want to be sure the date is okay with you."

How could I tell her no date would be good for me without Al being there?

The wedding took place about a year and a half after Al died. Janet's parents didn't have much money, so we split the cost three ways among them, Michael, and me. It was at Temple Beth El of Manhattan Beach, where I had attended my first meeting of the Metropolitan Branch of Women's League. How much had happened since then.

I wasn't very happy at the wedding (although you'd never know it – I put on a great face), but I was very happy with Janet. As wrong as Nancy may have been for Michael, that's how right Janet was.

When I think back on that situation and how it worked out, I am reminded of what happened to Helen Sussman. Her son, a student at Columbia at the time, asked if he could bring a date to a family party. The date was a young Chinese woman, a beautiful butterfly, who enchanted everyone.

Before you knew it, he was in love with her. Whereupon Helen and her husband Lou, a very successful accountant, decided to send their son to do graduate work in Italy, hoping the separation would end the romance.

It seemed everything was working out well, when the young man got into a serious accident. The parents flew to Italy and brought him back home.

One day, Helen went to visit her son in the hospital and found the Chinese girl there. Helen went right over to her and said, "This has nothing to do with you; you're a wonderful girl. But we could never accept you in our family. If you marry our son, we will have to exclude him. Please don't come here to see him again. You're not helping him; you're hurting him."

The girl never returned, and the boy's heart was broken. Afterwards, he wasn't the same. Time passed. He dated another Asian girl later, but by that time, Helen had died. He married the girl; they had a family. Lou has accepted the situation and apparently all are happy.

At the time, I thought Helen Sussman handled the situation properly. When it hit me personally, I wasn't so sure. Now I don't think she did the right thing at all.

With all that happened, the issue of my teaching at the same college as Michael no longer seemed to matter. I had told no one that Michael was my son. But when the list of faculty names and addresses was published in alphabetical order, everyone figured it out. I certainly wasn't his sister.

Then one day, a Marine Park neighbor, Abe Litke, got a hold of me. "Helen, you drive all the way into the city to teach at Manhattan Community College. Then you have to drive all the way back. The president of Kingsborough Community College would grab you in a minute. All I have to do is tell him I know you and you're good."

Abe was a professor of commercial law at Kingsborough, and what he said made sense. Kingsborough was maybe a fifteen-minute drive from Marine Park. So I agreed to let him set up an interview for me with Dr. Jacob Hartstein.

It went very well. We knew many of the same people, and he appeared most pleased with me. I was hired as an instructor, which, Dr. Hartstein explained, would put me on a tenure line. I was going through such a difficult time then that I wasn't even certain what "tenure" meant. But just like the word "matriculation" had sounded good to me years ago, "tenure" seemed something worthwhile.

In the fall of 1968 I began teaching at Kingsborough Community College. Classes were held in the former army barracks of Fort Tilden, located at the tip of Manhattan Beach. The magnificent seafront campus had yet to be built on this property, but the blueprint in the president's office showed what the college was going to look like, and it generated a tremendous sense of excitement. Dr. Hartstein's heart was set on having the most beautiful campus in the City University of New York – which, once completed, it arguably became – and he sought to save money on teachers' salaries and put it towards construction.

I found out about this the hard way. Several months into my teaching at Kingsborough, I got my contract. And it turned out that I had been hired not as an instructor but as a lecturer, a non-tenure-bearing line. It must be an error, I thought, and went into Dr. Hartstein's office to have it corrected. He lied right through his teeth. "I have it right here," he said. "We hired you as a lecturer."

Well, I was blown away. I couldn't believe anyone could be so false. But what could I do? Later on I became very friendly with Dr. Hartstein's secretary, May Pearlman, who told me that he had crossed out the word "instructor" on my contract and had replaced it with "lecturer." Apparently he did the same thing to several other people, and, as a result, he was ultimately called down to the Board of Higher Education and kicked upstairs. His replacement, a wise and kind man, reclassified me as an instructor. And I was on my way.

I truly loved my work. I had so many wonderful students who were very serious about getting an education. There were middle-class kids from Brooklyn neighborhoods. There were women who'd gotten married soon after high school, had children, and now were back in school. There were new immigrants determined to live out the American dream. There were minority students from poor backgrounds who wanted an education and the chance to move up. Kingsborough's student body was a real mixture of races, religions, social classes, young people just out of high school, and adults seeking to expand their knowledge or prepare for new careers. The very diversity of the students made it such an exciting environment.

Within a few years after I began teaching at Kingsborough, our new campus was complete. It was spread out over many acres with open lawns and secluded sitting areas, even its own private beach – a singularity among New York City colleges. The buildings were sparkling and new. Many windows overlooked the shoreline and the inlets of Jamaica Bay. Sitting in my own beautiful office with a water view, I thought of what my mother used to say: "If you live long enough, you'll get to see everything."

Although I was so happy with my public speaking and interpersonal communication courses, I dreaded teaching speech pathology. Every chairman I worked with understood this and kept it off my program. Then I ran into a problem with one of my colleagues. At that time, speech was part of a larger department that included theater, music, and art. Mary Crowley, a professor I was quite friendly with, approached me one day and said, "Helen, I'm going to run for chair of this department."

My face must have shown my reaction. I didn't think she would make a good chairman; I also didn't think she could win. "Mary," I said to her, "I can't let you do that. There are some very strong men in the department fighting to be chair. They will kill you."

"I can handle them," she said. "But I must count on your vote."

Well, I couldn't do that. I never promised to support her. And she did not win.

But the winner did appoint Mary deputy chair, and part of her job was to arrange the programs for all the speech professors. Here Mary had her revenge. She gave me several courses in pathology and, moreover, sent me to teach them in what I called "Siberia," an off-campus locale. I had some courses there and some on campus and had to drive back and forth. I had trouble parking off campus. In bad weather, it was a great hardship. This was a vindictive move on Mary's part and hard for me to forget.

We got a new president, Leon Goldstein. Ours was now the Department of Speech and Theater, and Leon, with whom I'd become quite friendly, told me he wanted to bring someone in from New York City Community College to head it up. Morty Becker would be an outstanding chairman, he said, and he urged me to get the others in the department to be welcoming to him.

I did as Leon asked. Morty may have heard about it, because we had a great relationship from the start. He was very good to me, very considerate of me as a widow and as a person in general. Morty would always accommodate me by giving me Wednesdays off, because that was the day Women's League National Board and Executive Board meetings were held, and I never, for a moment, gave up my involvement with Jewish organizational life, no matter how difficult it may have been.

At the same time, I was on ever so many committees at Kingsborough, because I wanted to move up the rungs. Then I decided that in order to do so, I would have to go back to college myself. The thought of going for a Ph.D. seemed too much, so I settled for another master's degree and enrolled in the popular broadcasting program at Brooklyn College.

After so many years, I was a night student again, working full time during the day. It was a marvelous experience although it wasn't easy. Both my sons had been good students when they were in college and it seemed I should do no less. So I found myself studying more diligently than ever.

An unusual thing that happened at that time was my developing a close friendship with a nun. Sister Elizabeth and I met in a debating course, where we were consistently assigned to opposite sides of an issue. Our major debate was about Taiwan. I argued it should be independent, but Sister Elizabeth, who had lived in Taiwan for a while and witnessed the terrible treatment of the people by the government, thought that it should be part of mainland China.

Although being back at college was most stimulating, I was not as impressed with Brooklyn College as I had been with NYU. Somehow Brooklyn seemed more provincial to me. Of course, I had enjoyed life so much more when I was a young student at NYU. Also, the level of students at Brooklyn was not as high.

This was around the time the open admissions policy was put into effect in the City University of New York, which guaranteed a place to any high school graduate. A consequence of the lowering of admission standards was a reduction in the overall academic ability of the student body. Still, I was very much in favor of open admissions, especially at the two-year colleges. I felt it gave an opportunity to introduce higher education to students who didn't have it all, allowing them the chance to begin to grapple with study. My view was in the minority; most of the professors were very much against open admissions, thinking it would lower the quality of the college. It did. But in my view, it was well worth it.

Open admissions brought many African American students into Kingsborough. At one point, one of my colleagues, Professor Sheldon Aptekar, had a confrontation with a young black woman, who accused him of racial bias. It became quite a cause célèbre in the college. A committee was appointed to try to straighten it out, but she refused to return to the class. Finally, Leon Goldstein called me into his office. "Please take her on. Teach her the course on a one-to-one basis," he said to me.

So I did. I think she misunderstood Professor Aptekar; she just had a little chip on her shoulder. But we got along quite well. Later on, when I heard of the independent studies that were offered in some of the elite colleges, I always thought back to the one that I had taught.

One September morning I was sitting at an orientation meeting at Kingsborough and, glancing around, I noticed a young man with piercing blue eyes who looked so familiar. Who can that be, I wondered. And then I realized it was Dennis Weintraub, the fellow in the placement office at NYU who nearly a decade ago had gotten me my first college teaching job at Manhattan Community College. I literally tripped over my feet to get to him.

"Dennis," I said, "what are you doing here?"

"I'm a new professor in the psychology department," he told me. "What are you doing here?"

We had a lot to catch up on.

A few years later, there was a fire on campus and a number of us had to temporarily double up on offices. Dennis Weintraub offered to share his office with me, and it worked out very well.

On an afternoon at the end of the semester, Dennis and I were sitting in our office when a young student of mine came in. "I must say goodbye to you before I go," Rebecca said and went on to tell me how much she enjoyed my class.

"Say goodbye to Professor Weintraub too," I said to Rebecca. "He's off to Israel to work on a dig."

"Oh," she said to him, "you must look up my cousin."

"I'm not interested in meeting anyone," he said, cutting her off abruptly.

I stepped in. "Write out your cousin's name and phone number on this piece of paper," I said to Rebecca. "I'll take care of it."

After she left, I bawled the hell out of him. "You stupid young man. You'll be working all week on your dig. Friday night will come around and you will want to be with a nice Jewish family and have a good Jewish meal. Here's your ticket." I took the piece of paper and put it in his pocket.

The next fall, Dennis came into the office with a lovely young woman. "Helen, meet Chana," he said. He had called Rebecca's cousin after all.

Today Dennis and Chana live in Be'er Sheva, where Dennis directs the adult education program of Ben-Gurion University, and Chana is secretary to its president. They have three sons. Whenever I see them, and I try to see them each time I'm in Israel, Dennis says to his sons, "If it wasn't for Helen, you wouldn't be here."

The first summer after Al Fried died, I didn't know what to do with myself. I was off from teaching and could have gone to the house in Copake. But without Al, it was somehow too painful. Then Charlotte Levine invited me to join her and her family in Israel.

Charlotte had had such a glorious time in Israel during our 1965 convention that she convinced Nathan to overcome his fear of flying in order to visit Israel with her the following year. We brought him to the airport, and I remember telling the other passengers in the lounge, "This is his first trip. Take care of him."

That one trip did it, and afterwards Charlotte and Nathan visited Israel many times. Ultimately they built a fantastic house in Herzelia Pituach. But this summer of 1968 they were renting a place in Netanya. Their five children and Charlotte's parents were coming along. There was room enough for me provided I shared a room with two of her teenage daughters.

One evening I was invited to the home of Zelda Kolitz, a prominent political figure, and there I met Chaim Landau, who was a leading member of the *Knesset* at that time. In the course of the evening, he learned I had never been to the *Knesset*, and he invited me to come down the next morning so he could show me around. Chaim was indeed giving me the royal tour. But he kept being interrupted. People were continuously coming over to him with questions. From what I could tell, there was some concern over an Algerian plane that had been seen flying over Israel. Finally I said, "Chaim, I'm sure your secretary can take me through. You have enough to do."

He gratefully agreed. His secretary, a sharp young woman, took over and gave me such a thorough tour there wasn't a thing I missed. The whole *Knesset* came alive before my eyes.

When it was over, I thanked her. "I know this was such a busy day. It was so good of you to spend all this time with me."

"Well," she said, "if you want to show any appreciation for this tour, I wish you would meet my best friend, Judith Apter. She is possessed about going to America. If you can help her in any way, that would be payment enough for me."

No sooner had I returned to Netanya when the phone rang. It was Judy Apter. She was ready to take me up on my offer to help her, she said, and wondered whether she and her mother could come over to meet me.

They arrived the very next day. Her mother was very possessive, reluctant to part with her lovely daughter. But after we chatted for a while, she said, "Now that I've met you, I feel comfortable about letting my girl go to America with you." I hadn't exactly offered her a place to live, but that's how it was interpreted.

So when I came home, Judy came along with me. She ended up living in my house for quite a few months. My mother was away during all that time, so she used Mama's room.

She was quite a personality, tall and attractive with long blonde hair that she kept flipping back from her face the way young women do nowadays. Later on Janet told me she was quite taken aback by Judy's presence. She and Michael were practically engaged at the time, and here I was bringing this attractive young woman to live with us, who could potentially be a threat to their relationship. Ultimately Judy and Janet became friends, but initially it must have come as a rude shock.

One day I returned home, and Judy greeted me, "Oh, Helen, you will never guess what happened. I met Elie Wiesel."

"Really," I said. "How did you get to him?"

"Oh, I went through your personal telephone book and found his name and number. I called him up. I told him I was your friend, and he invited me to come and visit him."

That was Judy. Ultimately I got her a job at a Jewish day school in New Jersey. It didn't work out, but that summer she went on a trip with some young people and ended up marrying one of the men who went along. She and her husband, Arthur Klinghoffer, are professors at Rutgers now, so all in all her coming to America worked out well.

Much as I mourned and missed Al Fried, I realized that I did not belong in the single world. So I developed a plan: if I didn't meet someone that I would want to marry, after being a widow for five years I would marry the first person I met, so long as he was right for me, my family, and my lifestyle, even if I didn't flip over him.

Four years had passed when a friend who belonged to the synagogue in Kew Garden Hills asked if I would be interested in meeting her rabbi. I had seen I. Usher Kirshblum and heard him speak. I knew he was an important public figure. But I also remembered he was short.

Still, I decided I would meet him. It was a lovely spring night. I took a taxi to Lou Siegal's kosher restaurant in Manhattan on the advice of my friend. "That way, he'll have to drive you home," she said.

Bells did not ring for me, but it was nevertheless a very nice evening. We had so much to talk about. As we were finishing dinner, Usher said to me, "I don't know if I'm imposing on you, but I'd like you to accompany me to a television taping. I'm being interviewed about the housing project in Forest Hills."

I had heard all about this. It was a big controversy at the time. There was a plan to build multiple housing for people of varied income levels in Forest Hills, and there were people in the neighborhood who objected vehemently. Usher was very vocal in his support for publicly supported housing. And I agreed with him; I felt there should be nice places for low-income people to live.

I agreed to go to the taping with him. We began talking about the issues involved, and I saw we were of one mind. When we got to the studio, Mario Cuomo, who was later to become governor of New York State, was there. The entire event was very exciting

That evening gave me my first glimpse into Usher's humanity, his commitment to help people. Even though no chemistry worked for me at that point, I sensed we shared common interests and ideals. I saw he was a committed person, and not only in terms of Jewish causes. I also noticed that his shirt was sparkling white. He had put himself together nicely.

In all the years I was a girl, my mother had never once waited up for me. This night I found her sitting at the kitchen table.

"Well, how did it go?"

"Okay."

"Will you see him again?"

"I don't know. Let's see if he calls."

He called very early the next morning and tied me down for another date.

IX

THE REBBETZEN OF KEW
GARDEN HILLS

I. USHER KIRSHBLUM was the youngest child of a very religious family that emigrated from Bialystok, Poland, when he was about eleven years old. They lived in the Borough Park section of Brooklyn, where his mother, who used to make shrouds, was known as a real *Aishet Chayil*. His older brother had become a distinguished rabbi, and Usher hoped to follow in his footsteps.

Mordecai Kirshblum was an Orthodox rabbi, however, while Usher became a Conservative rabbi. "I wear three epaulets on my shoulder," Usher used to say. "The first is the Orthodox, which I feel in my stomach, my lifestyle, and my background. The second is the Reform, because I was a graduate of the Jewish Institute of Religion. [This was the non-denominational seminary founded by the Reform Rabbi Stephen Wise, which has since merged with the Reform Hebrew Union College.] And the third is the Conservative, because I have always been a rabbi of a Conservative synagogue."

I had seen Usher at rabbinical conventions while I was president of Women's League, and I had noticed how much he stood out from the rest, how forceful he was, how committed to his ideals. Now, as we began going out together, the strength and determination of his character impressed me even further. Even if the entire community opposed him, he would not be dissuaded if he felt his position was correct, be it on a religious or secular matter. He was very involved in political issues as well.

But despite the fact that he often took unpopular stands, he was liked and admired by people in all branches of Judaism because he was so genuine. He was the first to come through with contributions and efforts for a cause he believed in. He had no *shticklach*. He was a humanistic sort of rabbi, compassionate, always ready to help. And he was also most elegant and eloquent in voice.

When Usher and I began seeing each other, his first wife had been dead for less than a year. Selma was an epileptic. Nevertheless, she led an active life, delivering speeches from time to time, as she was a fine public speaker. But then, in the midst of an address for the United Jewish Appeal, she suffered a seizure. It was a very traumatic event. Afterwards, she was no longer invited to speak in public, and that made her very unhappy.

Still, Usher was very devoted to her. He drove her everywhere. One day he came home to take her to the dressmaker. He called, "Selma, Selma." No answer. He went from room to room but could not find her. Finally he approached the stairway leading to the basement, and there was Selma lying at the foot of the stairs. Evidently an epileptic attack had caused the fall.

Her death was a terrible blow to him. Usher was despondent, inconsolable. He felt his life was over. People described him to me as a dying man. But a number of women in the congregation decided they weren't going to let that happen. They were going to find someone to bring him back to life. Time and again he told me, "You breathed a new breath into my life."

Our relationship developed very quickly. We set a date to be married once the first year after Selma's death had passed. My mother was thrilled with the news; so were my children. I did have some concern over whether Arthur and Michael would notice Usher's slight foreign accent. It bothered me a little at first; it seemed to lock him in my parents' European-born generation. But I had no cause for concern. Both my sons were Orthodox by the time I began seeing Usher, so they very much approved of his lifestyle.

Usher's son, Eliezer, was a cantor who lived in Toronto, and he and his wife, Linda, accepted me with great warmth. They had a baby boy and two little girls who couldn't understand why their grandmother wasn't around anymore and why I seemed to be taking her place, but they were delighted with me anyway. At one point, I was out walking with Risa, the older girl, who was about six or seven, when all of a sudden she stopped and took my hand. She looked up at me with those gorgeous big brown eyes and said, "What is a step-granddaughter? What am I a step to?"

"You're a step into my heart," I told her.

There was still Usher's daughter, Marsha, a single young woman who lived in Jerusalem. Usher said, "I must call Marsha. She'll be so happy." In my experience, it is the daughter who has difficulty accepting a replacement for her mother, and I tried to explain that to Usher. "Oh, no, Marsha will love you right away," he insisted.

The ice came through across the phone lines. "I hear you're looking around for another house," she said. "Why did I have to hear it from somebody else? What about my bedroom set?"

I understood. The house was part of her life. At the same time, I did not feel right moving into Usher's house. However beautifully decorated, it was the home he shared with another woman. "This house belongs to the synagogue," Usher had said to me. "If you want another house, I'll speak to the board about our moving."

In every synagogue there are those who love the rabbi and will do anything for him. In Usher's case, that group was quite large. He had been rabbi at Kew Garden Hills for almost all his adult life and was very much esteemed by the congregation. They said, "It's perfectly all right. We'll sell the house and get you another one." But when we started looking around at houses within walking distance of the synagogue, there wasn't one nearly as nice as the one Usher already had.

Usher then said, "Do whatever you like to this house." So I did. By the time I moved in, I had replaced Selma's bedroom set with my own and redecorated the entire house to suit my tastes.

Before we got married, we went to Jerusalem. The house situation was settled by then, and Marsha and I got to know each other. She came in for the wedding and all was well.

Rabbi Finkelstein performed the ceremony in the Seminary chapel. Because the space was so small, there was room only for family and very close friends. But what a thrill it was to be married in this exalted place that had become such an important part of my life, and by Rabbi Finkelstein, whom I so greatly admired.

We planned for the reception to be held in the garden behind Charlotte Levine's house, where a big tent had been set up. I envisioned people moving in and out of the tent and her beautiful garden on a lovely summer afternoon. But as it turned out, the morning of the wedding the skies opened up with such a heavy downpour the tent was not able to withstand it. The entire affair was picked up and moved to the Sands at Atlantic Beach. It was quite a crowd. With our joint families, the leadership from Usher's congregation, all our friends, and my associates from Women's League, we were over two hundred people.

I sold the house in Marine Park. After the movers left and I closed the door for the last time, I stopped and thought about this quiet Brooklyn neighborhood where I'd spent so many years, going back to the time my parents bought the house brand new and I was still a young woman living at home. This was where I shared a life with Al Fried, where my children were born and grew up, where I first became involved with the Sisterhood of the Marine Park Jewish Center, which led to my life in Women's League and my connection to the Seminary. But soon I broke my reverie. I have always looked forward, and now was the time to begin a new life.

Since I became active in the Conservative movement, I had placed myself in its liberal wing. Usher, although he was the rabbi of a Conservative synagogue, was Orthodox in his personal lifestyle. I would have to adjust my observance of Judaism to match his. That meant reading food labels to make sure they met kosher standards, and stricter Sabbath observance to the extent of not even switching lights on or off.

A big test came the first time I was to attend *Shabbat* services as Usher's wife. A few days earlier, I noticed that the weather forecast called for rain Saturday, and as I have always believed I would melt in the rain, I told Usher I would carry an umbrella to walk up the single block to the *shul* on Main Street. "Helen, dear," Usher said very kindly to me – he always spoke very kindly to me – "you can't carry an umbrella. It's not permitted. People in this community don't carry umbrellas on *Shabbat*."

"Why not?"

"Because it is viewed as opening something like a tent. You're not allowed to do that."

"Okay," I said. "If that's the case, I'll open the umbrella on Friday afternoon and leave it on the porch. That way I won't be opening it on Saturday."

"Oh no, dear," Usher said. "People will think you opened it on Saturday. It is the principle of *marit ayin* – how it looks to the eye."

This was a dilemma. No way was I about to have the smart suit and flowered hat I planned to wear ruined by the rain. Yet I could not go against Usher's wishes. Finally I thought of a solution. I got a big plastic cover that shielded me from head to toe, and thus protected I walked to *shul*.

But if I adjusted to Usher's stricter standards of observance, he adjusted his standards to mine in terms of dining out. Previously he wouldn't enter a restaurant that wasn't specifically kosher. Now, to please me, he would go to restaurants where he could have a meal of fish and vegetables.

Early on in our marriage we were visiting a European city, and I convinced Usher to eat in the hotel restaurant. He was served some kind of quiche that looked to be all right. But as he began to eat it, he tasted something suspect. It turned out the quiche was made with bacon.

I never saw him so disturbed. It was as if he were going directly to hell for this transgression. "This is the last time I will ever eat in a nonkosher restaurant," he declared.

I did not say a word. I know if somebody is terribly disturbed, the best thing to do is keep quiet, walk into another room if possible, give him the chance to cool off. How did I learn this? Not from my mother certainly. My father never raised his voice to her. It was instinctive. Somehow I knew if I kept quiet, it would blow over.

Afterwards we never spoke of the incident. And Usher did continue to eat in nonkosher restaurants. But he was very, very careful.

Before I married Usher, I had the impression that Queens was a place of cemeteries. Now I began to appreciate the warm and beautiful communities of the borough. Kew Garden Hills, in particular, was such a nice Jewish community. The women were very respectful to me. They knew I was teaching full time and very involved in my own volunteer work, and therefore they didn't expect a full time *rebbetzen*. But somehow I became one anyway.

Nowadays rabbis' wives dislike the word *rebbetzen*, but I always liked it. I felt a *rebbetzen* could assist the rabbi more than anyone else and I was determined to do my best. I initiated a *Shabbat* event I called "T&T" for "Tea and Talk," where I'd invite the women and their husbands, if they were so inclined, to our home on Saturday afternoons for a couple of hours of discussion, accompanied by tea and cakes, nuts and fruits. The idea was based on the salons I had witnessed as a little girl in my grandfather's home, and with that as my model, I saw to it that we never indulged in idle conversation, but discussed current events and Jewish-related subjects.

One of the more unusual T&Ts was when Sister Elizabeth joined us. I had invited her for *Shabbat*, and Saturday morning we attended services together. "I don't think it would be proper for me to walk into the synagogue with my veil," Sister Elizabeth had said. Although she dressed in modern fashion, she did wear a short veil.

"That's okay," I said. "I'll give you a hat."

So she replaced her veil with a lovely white flowered hat, put her cross inside her dress, and walked to *shul* with me. At the T&T, the women were delighted to meet her. She was a great, remarkable lady, with a broad Irish face and sense of humor to match, so interested in the way we lived and what we were about. I think she learned a lot about Judaism that weekend.

As Usher's wife, I learned a lot about Judaism as well. The first year of our marriage, as we moved past the High Holy Days and on to *Sukkoth*, I discovered how important this eight-day festival was. Particularly I came to see what a great responsibility it presented to a rabbi's wife.

We prepared the *sukkah* on the large terrace outside our breakfast room, hanging vines, flowers, and dried fruits from a makeshift roof frame. After the first two holy days, I went to work, came home, and prepared a dinner for anywhere from twelve to twenty people, using my fine china and best tableware, with no outside help except for the women in the community.

But I established a routine that first *Sukkoth*, and it became the standard for all the years of my life with Usher. The menu was soup, followed by chicken and brisket. As I served today's brisket, tomorrow's was simmering in a very slow oven. Of course, all our meals had to be eaten outdoors in the *sukkah*. When it rained, we joked that the soup portions were a little bigger.

While the menu never varied, the guest list did. We had family one night, friends the next night, board members the night after that. It worked out fine except that poor Usher had to eat the same meal every night for an entire week.

Sukkoth had become a new responsibility in my life. Passover, on the other hand, had become a liberation. I always said Usher liberated me from two things: Passover and graduate school. When it came to graduate school, now that Usher was supporting me, I no longer had the pressure to move up the academic ladder in order to earn more. I still had a thesis to do, which was no problem. But I also had one course to take, statistics, and that was enough of a drawback for me to decide to give up the whole thing.

As for Passover, Usher had arranged with his congregation that he would forfeit some vacation time in order to be free to spend this holiday with his family in Israel. He argued that *Pesach* is not a holiday for the synagogue as much as it is for family and friends.

I concurred. Al Fried and I had had so many wonderful *sedarim* for our family and friends in Marine Park. At one time during my Women's League presidency, *The World Telegram and Sun* sent a crew out to our home and did a terrific story with photographs on capturing the essence of the *seder*.

But making *Pesach* is an enormous job that requires a complete kitchen overhaul: cleaning out all the cupboards and drawers and changing all the dishes, pots, pans, silverware, and table linens. So it was without much difficulty that I gave it all up in favor of celebrating Passover with Usher's family in Jerusalem. Marsha was in Jerusalem. So was Mordecai, who had made *aliyah* years before. And then Susan and Arthur made *aliyah* with their family. So it was very fulfilling for me to live out the mandate that concluded our *sedarim* in the Diaspora: "Next year in Jerusalem."

Usher and I may have celebrated Passover in Jerusalem, but we celebrated *Shabbat* every week in Kew Garden Hills. As Usher's wife, I attended services regularly. As a speech professor, I took a professional interest in the way he prepared his sermons. Usually he would take the portion of the week and apply it to contemporary life and current issues. He would write the theme of his address on the top of an index card and list four main ideas underneath. That was all he wrote down. But I saw how he spent hours thinking through what he was going to say. When he delivered his sermons, he appeared so confident that one might think they were prepared with ease. Only he and I knew how much effort he put into every one of them.

Marsha always found Usher's style too schmaltzy. My children tended to agree. But to me, the emotionalism in his language, the depth of his ideas, and his impassioned delivery were very moving. I thought he was an outstanding speaker whose message and delivery were absolutely right for his audience.

Up on the *bimah*, Usher was very serious and professional in his demeanor. But when Michael and Janet's daughters, Rachel and Miriam, stayed over for *Shabbat*, and I brought them to services with me, they would run up onto the *bimah*, and Usher would absolutely melt. The little girls loved coming to our home Friday night, sleeping over, and spending *Shabbat* with us. The foyer in our house led to a sunken living room. They transformed it into a stage for impromptu performances, as they dressed in Nanny's clothes, hats, and high-heeled shoes. With Michael and Janet's two daughters and Arthur and Susan's five daughters (eventually there would be six), my long ago dream of having a little girl had come true in abundance. I felt truly blessed.

Arthur and Susan had one boy as well. In marrying me, Usher ultimately got nine additional grandchildren. He was the only grandfather they ever knew, and they loved him dearly.

They also knew and loved a great-grandmother, even though by this time my mother lived in Florida and Arizona for most of the year. Then she fell ill, was over medicated, and I had to bring her back to New York. We set up a hospital bed in the living room. It was very difficult for me. I was working full time, busy with an active congregation, and my mother required a great deal of attention.

I shared my concerns with Usher, but it wasn't until I was away for a day and Usher was left alone with her that he realized just how difficult it was. "You are right, Helen," he said to me. "We'll have to find another living arrangement for Mother."

We found a nursing home in Far Rockaway, run by people we knew. They took excellent care of her. Nevertheless and even though she never said a word, I knew she didn't want to be there. Until she died, I'd visit her every day after teaching, driving from Kingsborough to Far Rockaway, and then back to Kew Garden Hills. I saw how unhappy she was, and it would kill me.

My mother's illness and subsequent death were difficult to bear. But overall, my life with Usher was a very happy one, enriched by some very fine people in the congregation.

When I first came across the names David and Dora Levine, it brought to mind my father's customer David Levine, whose wife's name was also Dora. I used to keep the books for his buttonhole business, and whenever I billed David Levine, my father would comment on how nice a man he was.

Now, I wondered, could this possibly be the same David Levine? Yes it was, and all the things my father had said about him were true. Anyone in the dress business at that time would recognize the name David Levine. He manufactured very high quality women's clothing. When I was about to marry Usher, he insisted I come up to his factory and select a dress for the wedding. I ended up selecting two.

David Levine was enormously kind to Usher. Every year before the High Holidays, he would insist that Usher get a new suit and overcoat, sending him to the finest tailors to be outfitted. Usher was one of the best-dressed rabbis around.

Other congregants were generous to Usher as well. Before I was in the picture, a man who owned a computer company asked Usher to be its treasurer and gave him a lot of stock. The value of the stock rose. At one point, Usher thought to sell it all, but the congregant said, "Look at it like a cow that gives milk. It will give more milk and more milk and more milk." Ultimately the milk ran out, but before it did, Usher's financial situation improved enormously.

There was nothing unusual about such practices. Rabbis' salaries were generally dismal back then, especially in Queens and Brooklyn. They enhanced their earnings through officiating at weddings and funerals. Also congregants typically gave them gifts, often of things the rabbis couldn't use and didn't want. To this day I have more *challah* covers and *kiddush* cups than I know what to do with. I would have preferred fewer gifts and a better salary.

But there were substantial benefits. The house was owned and paid for by the congregation. People in the garment business, like David Levine, saw to it that Usher and I got our clothing wholesale when they were not outright gifts. Usher always drove a late model Cadillac, courtesy of a dealership-owning congregant. There was always a deal for the rabbi.

Such material perks were part of the picture. The more important perk to me, however, was getting to know the many distinguished, accomplished people who were part of Usher's circle. Because he could reach out so beautifully, Usher had a wide circle of friends from non-Jewish as well as Jewish life, among them political, theatrical, and academic, as well as religious figures.

Menachem Begin was a close personal friend. Time and again Usher would talk about him as a great historic figure. Begin was so brilliant, Usher would say, that when he spoke, people would hang on his every word. I must have seen pictures of him in the newspapers and on television, but somehow Usher's description left me with the impression that Begin was a tall and handsome man.

Then we were invited to a reception given in his honor at a magnificent home in Great Neck, Long Island. It was a gathering of major donors, what we called the heavy hitters, and by the time we arrived, a substantial crowd had already gathered.

As soon as we entered, a short and most unattractive man at the opposite end of the living room got up and strode purposefully towards us. Who is this guy, I wondered.

Before even greeting Usher, he took my hand and kissed it – first on the back, then on the palm, while looking directly into my eyes. It was only when he began speaking that I realized this was Menachem Begin. Usher introduced us, and the two men fell into conversation, whereupon I got as far away from them as possible and spent the entire evening at the other end of the room.

On the way home, I shared my disagreeable impression of Begin with Usher, concluding with the comment: "He's a womanizer."

"Oh, Helen dear," Usher said, "you've got him so wrong. He's continental. That's the way men who come from that part of Europe behave when they meet a woman."

Needless to say, Usher was right, and my first impression was as wrong as could be. Later on I got to know Begin and his wife quite well. I visited him many times, even at the official residence in Jerusalem, when he had become prime minister. As Usher often said, Begin was a great man, a humanist, a truly beautiful person.

There were no false first impressions of Jan Peerce, however. The famed tenor was a close friend of Usher's as well. Although it was hardly on the level of Jan Peerce's, Usher's singing voice was quite pleasing, and whenever we got together, the two men would sing together, usually old Yiddish songs and prayers, while I accompanied them on the piano.

At one time, when Jan Peerce was in Los Angeles visiting his daughter, he fell ill and had to be hospitalized. A *Lubavitcher* came to visit him and was so inspiring and encouraging about his recovery that he won him over. After that, Jan Peerce became enamored with the *Lubavitch* movement and decided that he wanted to be able to entertain members of this group in his home. In order to do that, his wife Alice had to have their home rekoshered in accordance with *Lubavitch* requirements. It was a tremendous undertaking, and Usher was very helpful in advising them on what had to be done.

I saw *Fiddler on the Roof* quite a few times, but never was it as moving as when Jan Peerce played Tevye. He may not have had the comic gusto of a Zero Mostel, but his voice was incomparable. It was late in the Broadway run when Jan Peerce took over the role. His eyes were so bad at that time, they had to mark the places on the stage where he was to stand. He told me that finding his place was far more difficult than singing the songs.

To me, *Fiddler* was an important indication of how much Eastern European Jewish life had impacted on the American culture. I had loved musical theater from the time my mother used to schlep me along to the Yiddish theater when I was a child. Or if she didn't take me along, she'd bring home the sheet music for me to play on the piano. But Sholem Aleichem's story, enhanced by songs like "Sunrise, Sunset," became a classic that told our story to audiences all over the world.

The years that I was married to Usher were times of great transformation. In New York, there was a financial crisis, fewer city services, an increase in drug use, theft, and violence. We were robbed twice during that period. The first time was when we came home from a United Synagogue Convention to find the house ransacked. All my beautiful hats were turned inside out and dumped on the bed with their linings ripped out. Evidently the robbers had some thought that women hide jewelry in their hats. I, however, had so little thought of being robbed, that I didn't bother to hide anything. The robbers had more luck going directly to my jewelry box, where they found a strand of cultured pearls alongside a strand of Mallorca pearls. They were clever enough to recognize the difference and leave the Mallorca pearls behind.

The second time we were robbed was potentially a far more dangerous situation. We were home and asleep. Marsha was visiting at the time. Although she had a habit of falling asleep on the couch downstairs in front of the television, luckily this night she was in her bed. I don't know how we slept through everything. But the next morning, we came downstairs to find a house that looked like it had been hit by a tornado.

This time the thieves took household things: a lot of silver, paintings, and an antique clock with chimes, which had been a wedding gift from my sister, Nettie, to Usher and me. I missed that greatly.

A few days later, the caretaker of the synagogue, a man who always seemed so friendly and delightful, left the job without notice. No one ever saw or heard from him again. I always believed that he masterminded both robberies.

There was a breakdown of law and order during this era, but there was also an opening up of society, which I approved of in large measure. The civil rights movement and the marches and protests against the Vietnam War stimulated groups of people like homosexuals, Native Americans, and the handicapped to argue for greater equality. The feminist movement was part of this tide of protest, and its effects were being felt in certain Jewish quarters.

Among Conservative and Reform Jews, it emerged in a movement to allow women a greater role in synagogue rituals. There were those who believed women should be counted for a *minyan*, that they should be given *aliyot*, even that they should be admitted to the rabbinate. As I spoke at conferences on behalf of Women's League and the Seminary, I was witness to these demands.

In my heart, I felt women should have a greater role in synagogue religious life. There was no *halachic* ruling against women being called to the *Torah*, being part of a *minyan*, or even being a rabbi. Usher, however, was vehemently against such changes. He believed there was an important role for women in Judaism. He was all for women being educated to *daven* and to study Jewish history, ritual, and law. But to him, the woman was the crux of the Jewish family; it fell to her to set the example of Jewish life in the home.

A distinguished committee, composed of men for the most part, but lay people as well as rabbis, was appointed at the Seminary to explore the issue of women being allowed to become rabbis. Chancellor Gerson Cohen, Louis Finkelstein's successor, urged Usher to campaign against it. "We can't do what you can do. You have an organization [the Rabbinical Assembly]."

Usher was in the forefront of the Union for Traditional Conservative Judaism, a group that moved away from the main body in protest. They argued there was no *halachic* basis for such a change.

Although we never discussed these issues, I think Usher had a sense of how I felt. But I never confronted him. In my lectures I skimmed over the subject. My reasoning was, it didn't get in my way, whereas it was a major part of his identity.

I had decided to play it very cool.

X

JOURNEYS WITH USHER

As USHER LOVED TO TRAVEL, we went on many trips during our life together. They were never just vacations, however, but always connected to some larger purpose. Usher was driven to see how Jews were living today and how they had lived in the past in many parts of the world. Our most frequent destination, of course, was Israel. There were times we visited Israel as often as five times a year.

Members of our family lived there. Also Usher attended the World Zionist Congress in Jerusalem whenever it was in session, which included representatives from all branches of the Zionist movement throughout the Diaspora. At first I accompanied him as his spouse, and after his death I continued to attend as a delegate in my own right.

A particularly memorable trip was when Michael and his family came with us. Years before, when Michael was close to being bar mitzvahed, Al Fried and I had told him, "You can have the same kind of party Arthur had, or you can have a trip to Israel."

Michael said, "Oh, I'd rather go to Israel."

So the day of his bar mitzvah we had a nice lunch at the synagogue after services, and that night Michael had a party for his friends. But we never seemed to find the time to keep our word and take Michael to Israel. Either he was in school, or Al was too busy at work, or we were away for the summer at Copake.

Finally, I did keep my word. Only by then Michael was a grown man, and Janet and two-year-old Rachel were part of the belated bar mitzvah package.

In the late 1970s, Usher kept the promise he had made to himself and visited his home city of Bialystok. For years the political climate made Bialystok an unlikely destination for American Jews, but by the 1970s, travel to Eastern Europe was becoming more common.

In 1978 Hanka and Aaron Lew, congregants and neighbors whose backyard adjoined ours, decided to go to Poland, so that Hanka could visit the gravesite of her father in Lodz. Hanka asked if Usher and I would like to go along with them and another couple, cousins of theirs.

As Bialystok was not far from Lodz, Usher thought this might be the right time for such a trip. But he had doubts about visiting a country whose Jewish population had been so thoroughly devastated, and he decided to seek the advice of Rabbi Menachem Schneerson, the *Lubavitcher Rebbe*, in his headquarters at 770 Eastern Parkway in Brooklyn. Although not a follower per se, Usher was devoted to the *Rebbe* and often went to him with his concerns. At the *farbringens* the *Rebbe* would spot Usher and call him up. One of the rabbis there would get so upset to see Usher, a Conservative rabbi, being recognized, that he would get up and walk out of the room.

This time, when Usher was called up, he told the *Rebbe* about the projected trip and his doubts. "From what I've heard, there are so few Jews left in Poland," Usher said. "How will I be able to find them?"

"Don't worry," the *Rebbe* answered. "You will be wearing your *yarmulke*. The Polish Jews will find you." And he encouraged Usher to make the trip.

So with the blessings of the *Rebbe*, we decided to go. Our first destination was Warsaw, where we could not help but be impressed with the tourist sites, like the magnificent opera house. But they were not the real subjects of our visit. We viewed our trip as a pilgrimage to discover what was left of the vibrant Jewish community that had existed in this country for centuries.

At one point, we were in a lovely restaurant where I struck up a conversation with a waiter. After we chatted pleasantly for a while, I said to him, "How about the anti-Semitism here?"

He looked me straight in the eye and said, "Yes, the red wine is better."

That was one of the first indications we had that this trip was not going to be successful. We did manage to find the site of the Warsaw Ghetto, which today is a major public destination and appropriately marked. In 1978, however, there was nothing more than a street sign to acknowledge its existence. People passed by without a second glance.

Our next stop was Lodz. It wasn't until many years later, when people started to get into genealogy, that a cousin told me my mother's parents had come from Lodz. Had I known when I was there, I would have tried to research where they were born and had grown up. I would have tried to discover if anyone from their families was left. But even if I had such information, it would not have gotten me very far.

For years Hanka had been sending money to a gentile couple who were supposed to be caring for her father's gravesite. Yet they were nowhere to be found. We did find the cemetery, but it was in a terrible state of disrepair and desecration. (It has since been repaired and restored by the Lodzers – a group of American Jews with roots in Lodz.) We saw a mausoleum that belonged to the Poznansky family, owner of the biggest garment factory in Lodz. It was known for its beautiful stained-glass windows. All were smashed. Glass debris littered the ground. Monuments were toppled over, hidden beneath weeds.

In this sad environment, the six of us searched and searched for Hanka's father's grave to no avail. Finally Usher said to Hanka, "Let us just accept the fact that where we are standing at this moment is where your father is buried," and he prepared to say the prayer over the grave closest at hand.

Just then, Hanka brushed the leaves off another tombstone with her foot. Unbelievably it was her father's. It was an extraordinary discovery, but it could not mitigate the larger pain.

We went on to Auschwitz, which was not yet the museum it has become. Still, we saw the barracks with the boards people slept on, the gas chambers, the crematoria, the Birkenau work camp, all unbelievably horrifying sights. To Hanka and Aaron, who were survivors, it brought back a nightmare that was all too real.

Hanka was only fifteen years old when she and her mother were taken to Auschwitz. They were standing on the selection line, and Hanka saw what looked like an important Nazi official at the head, indicating which people should go to the left or to the right. It was the infamous Dr. Mengele.

When they reached the head of the line, her mother was sent off in one direction. Hanka tried to follow her, but Mengele pulled her back to go in the other direction. She had a rash on the inside of her thigh and kept her knees pressed together to prevent it from being seen, fearing something terrible would be done to her if it were noticed.

Hanka's mother was sent off to be gassed; she herself was sent to Birkenau where she managed to survive. The last image of her mother on the selection line, she told us, is emblazoned on her memory forever.

After the war, Hanka told us, she was reluctant to talk about her experiences. Years later she realized it was her obligation to speak about them if she could. Like many survivors, she goes to schools and community centers reliving the horrors of her past, so that future generations will know what happened.

From Lodz we went on to Bialystok. Usher had managed to locate a man who claimed to be the single remaining Jew in that city. They set up a time and place to meet, but the man never showed up. We did find Usher's childhood home, but the door was locked and the window shades pulled firmly down. As we walked around the house, a woman lifted a shade, glared at us in a most unpleasant manner, and quickly snapped it shut.

Bialystok, the birthplace of Jews like Ludwig Zamenhof, who invented the international language Esperanto, and Albert Sabin, who invented the oral polio vaccine, was to all appearances *Judenrein* (free of Jews). The Great Synagogue, built in 1908 and among the grandest in Eastern Europe, had been burned by the Nazis in June 1941, with two thousand Bialystok Jews inside. The remaining Jewish population was herded into the Bialystok Ghetto, accompanied by the jeering of many Poles.

Two years later, when they heard of the Warsaw Ghetto uprising, the Bialystok Jews formed a resistance unit. But their rebellion was quickly crushed, and forty thousand survivors were shipped to Auschwitz and Maidanek. It was not until 1993, fifteen years after our visit, that an obelisk was erected on the grounds of the ghetto cemetery, dedicated to the Bialystok Jewish martyrs.

Ironically, while we were in Poland, a number of Yiddish-related events were going on. There was a Yiddish theater group in Warsaw, made up of primarily non-Jews by the way, that was highly thought of. But our feeling was that it represented a community and culture that no longer had any life, any vibrancy. For all these reasons, our trip turned out to be a most heart-wrenching experience, and we left Poland feeling we would never return.

Back home Usher visited the *Lubavitcher Rebbe* and told him how disappointing our trip had been, how no Jews had approached us; indeed, we could not even find any Jews. But the *Rebbe* was not convinced our journey was in vain. "It doesn't have to be apparent at the moment," he said to Usher. "You don't know how much good you have done." That may have been true. My memory of Poland, however, remains tinged with sorrow and anger.

A few years later a trip to Morocco left us with entirely different feelings and far happier memories. Usher had been interested in seeing the Sephardic communities in this Moslem nation that dated back to the time of the expulsion from Spain in 1492, when many Jews found sanctuary in the lands of the Ottoman Empire.

He asked Rabbi Isaac Trainin and his wife, Frances, to join us, and before we left, the executive director of the Joint Distribution Committee sent word of the imminent arrival of two prominent American rabbis. As a result, every door was opened, and the red carpet – a beautiful Moroccan one at that – was rolled out.

We had a driver who took us from Rabat to Casablanca and to many places in between. The environment was so exotic, and I was enchanted by the domed roofs and Mudejar arches, the blue and white tiled walls, the fountains and pools to be found in even the smallest of gardens, and the people dressed in flowing robes and caftans. We were told that a good number of the poorer Moroccan Jews had emigrated to Israel, while the ones who were well off remained behind.

One *Shabbat* we were invited to the home of a very prosperous Jewish man, the owner of a big olive oil business. We were seated close to the ground on benches covered with satin cushions and having an excellent dinner of couscous, lamb kebobs, and fish, when suddenly Usher began to choke on a fish bone. It was terrifying; I thought he would actually choke to death. But our host tore a piece of *challah* into little balls and stuffed them, one after the other, down Usher's throat. Incredibly, this method succeeded in dislodging the bone. It was a remedy I never forgot.

The next to the last day we were there, we visited the home of a Moroccan *chassid*. A relatively young man, he had come to Morocco with his wife, where he was building up a family and a community. I found it amazing. The Sephardic and Ashkenazic traditions are so different. Yet these *Lubavitchers* were drawing people.

We enjoyed spending time in his happy household and were about to leave when he asked me, "Is there anything you wanted to buy here?"

"Well," Usher interjected, "Helen was looking around for a caftan that seemed authentically Moroccan. But she didn't find anything."

The *chassid* turned to me. "Tomorrow morning, I'll pick you up and take you to a place where you'll find just what you like."

Sure enough, the next morning, he was at the hotel. He took me where tourists never go, and there I found a black caftan woven through with gold threads. As I was trying it on, I heard the *chassid* say, "Tell her to come out. I want to see how it looks on her."

He approved. "Very nice," he said, adding, "Don't ask about the price. I'll handle it."

Our trip to South America was of a different order. This time Rabbi Mordecai Waxman and his wife, Ruth, from Great Neck, New York, joined us along with about forty congregants from Conservative synagogues across the country – under the aegis of the World Council of Synagogues – to visit and to learn more about Jewish communities throughout South America.

The time we spent in Buenos Aires was perhaps the most memorable segment of the trip. There was great unrest in Argentina at that time. Young people disappeared overnight; many were Jewish. "Missing" became the code word. People appealed to us to spread the word when we returned, but there was little we could do.

We were warned it was dangerous. We were told not to walk alone. One man in our group was robbed not once, but twice.

Still, Buenos Aires was a fascinating city, and the growth of its Conservative movement, because of Rabbi Marshall Meyer, was of great interest to us. I remembered Marshall Meyer as a young, charismatic seminarian in New York. He was the son of John Meyer of Norwich, Connecticut, a well-known and well-to-do women's clothing manufacturer.

When he was about to graduate, the Buenos Aires community asked the Jewish Theological Seminary to send them a Conservative rabbi, and for some reason Marshall Meyer volunteered to go. He thrived there even though he didn't speak Spanish. He was such a dynamic, vital personality that he whipped up that community. People said it was Rabbi Marshall Meyer who had virtually brought Conservative Judaism to Buenos Aires, drawing a thousand young people every *Shabbat* and establishing Argentina's first Conservative *seminario*.

This was the time Jacob Timmerman, Argentina's renowned Jewish newspaper editor, was imprisoned for his antigovernment stance. Marshall Meyer would visit him in prison every day. Because he made no secret of his hatred of the fascist government, his activism resulted in his life being threatened. That was when he packed up his family and came to New York, where he took over the rabbinate of B'nai Jeshurun, transforming that Upper West Side synagogue from a dormant institution into the active, rousing congregation it remains to this day. Luckily for us, however, Marshall Meyer was still in Buenos Aires during our visit, so we could see firsthand what he had accomplished, and we could enjoy the beautiful chorale program he organized in our honor.

My single frightening experience in Buenos Aires had nothing to do with the political situation. It happened one *Shabbat* morning when I urged Usher to leave for services without me. He liked to go early in order to have the opportunity to speak to people. "Go ahead," I said. "I'll find my way to *shul*."

My sense of direction has never been good. From the minute I was born, I think, I didn't know which way to go. But then I found my way and have been going ever since.

So I felt very confident about getting to the synagogue on my own. But as it turned out, I couldn't find anyone early in the morning who could speak a word of English. I went into store after store, trying to communicate by gesture, putting my hands together as if in prayer, hoping people would understand.

But no one did. I was lost for the longest time. I couldn't even find my way back to the hotel. I nearly panicked. Finally, one storekeeper seemed to understand my gesture. "Church?" he asked.

I vehemently shook my head, "Yes, yes, Jewish, Jewish." He took me by the hand and walked me to the synagogue.

But there was another incident during this South American trip where a nonverbal gesture nearly got me in trouble. This was when we were in Brazil, and a site I had hoped to visit was deleted from our tour, because the guide felt there wouldn't be enough time.

The tour was nearly over when the guide approached me. "You know, I think we are going to be able to squeeze that site in," she said.

"That's great!" I told her and spontaneously raised my hand, forming an "O" with my thumb and middle finger.

"My goodness," she cried, "don't do that."

"What did I do?"

"That sign you made – any man who sees it will think you're inviting him to go to bed."

"Really?"

"Yes," she added, "and if a gentleman nearby straightens his tie, it means he accepts."

Well, I thought, putting on my speech professor's cap for the moment, the next time I teach nonverbal communication, I will have to tell my students how so innocuous a gesture in our culture could be so provocative in Brazil.

In March 1982 Usher received an invitation from the government of Taiwan to be part of a group of twelve North American clergymen, one of three rabbis, along with Rabbi Waxman and Rabbi Max Lipschitz of North Miami, to participate in what they called the American Interfaith Delegation to the Republic of China. The purpose of the trip was to expose the clergymen to the wonders of Taiwan, to enhance its image, and consequently to increase its tourism.

We were flown first class on Republic of China Airways. I have yet to experience air travel as elegant and luxurious. The plane was like a big living room, the service beyond what I ever expected or hoped to see.

In Taiwan we met with the president and cabinet ministers. Their wives were there as well, all beautiful women wearing dresses of fine silk brocade with mandarin collars and double strands of eight-millimeter pearls.

I became friendly with the wife of a minister whom everyone said was slated to become the next president of Taiwan. At one point she told me she had lived in Brooklyn for a while and worked at the big library on Eastern Parkway. Was I familiar with it, she wanted to know.

"Oh yes," I said. "In fact my daughter-in-law lives nearby, and she takes her six children there all the time." Susan loved that area: the library, the Brooklyn Museum, and the Botanical Gardens.

"Just a minute," she said to me, "can their name be Fried?"

She was able to describe Susan and all the kids to me. It was so amazing. I go all the way to Taiwan and meet a woman who knows my family.

Before we left for Taiwan, Usher had written ahead describing our dietary requirements in great detail. Nevertheless, on the gigantic lazy

Susan that was brought out for our first dinner, the section reserved for us contained shellfish. When Usher explained we could not eat such foods, he was invited into the kitchen to select an appropriate fish, which they then promised to prepare for us.

A short time later, an elaborate platter was presented. In the center was the fish, grilled to perfection – only it was surrounded by shrimps. It had to go back again. Ultimately they got it right, and in the meanwhile we had many small vegetarian dishes that staved off any hunger.

When Sister Elizabeth learned we would be going to Taiwan, she asked me to look up her friend who, she said, was unjustly imprisoned. She hoped I would try to arrange for his release, and she urged me to speak out, as an American educator, against the abuses of human rights. But I was a guest of the government. It was not possible or prudent for me to do anything of that nature.

Once we came home, however, we all agreed we could not fulfill the mission our hosts envisioned. They wanted us to become public relations spokespeople extolling the wonders of Taiwan. And while we certainly could speak about the beautiful objects of art and great architecture that we saw and the royal treatment we received, we could not speak well of the political environment. Taiwan was certainly no democracy.

After leaving Taiwan, Usher and I went on to Tokyo. That Saturday we attended services in a synagogue divided into three sections: to the left of the *bimah* was the portion reserved for the Orthodox, in the center was the portion reserved for the Conservative, and on the right was the portion reserved for the Reform. There I noticed a Japanese woman, very elegantly dressed in western style. Julie Maltzman, the rabbi's wife, told me she was the widow of one of the more active members of this congregation. While they lived together, she began to feel closer to Judaism. After he died, she converted in order to be able to be buried beside her husband.

Rabbi Jonathan Maltzman was spending this early part of his career in Tokyo and invited Usher and me to his home for *Shabbat* dinner. During the evening, I realized I had met Jonathan's parents when I spoke before his father's congregation in Santurce, a section of San Juan, Puerto Rico. At that time, his mother told me Jonathan had recently come home from school and asked, "Mommy, is it true that I killed Jesus Christ?" Shortly afterwards the Maltzmans returned to the mainland United States.

I had taken a salami along with us on this trip to the Far East thinking there might be a time when we might want to have meat and would not be able to find anything suitable. This long salami had accompanied us all the way to Taiwan and on to Tokyo. Now, as it was close to the end of our journey, I took the salami, wrapped it very nicely, and brought it to the Maltzman home.

"I have a gift for you," I said to Julie. And I handed her this long, narrow package.

She looked at it curiously. "Go on, open it," I said.

"Oh my," she exclaimed happily. "We haven't had salami in such a long time."

The world's longest traveling salami had finally found a home.

In early spring of the following year we were on the road again, this time to Florida, where we planned to visit Usher's sister, Chana, who was quite ill. He was concerned he might not see her again. That turned out to be true, but not in the way we expected.

We arrived at my sister Nettie's home on a Thursday evening. Nettie was a widow now and living in a beautiful apartment in Margate, Florida, which she had decorated so magnificently that it was the talk of the town. In order to give a sense of space to her tiny entrance foyer, she paneled all the walls and the ceiling with mirrors. That was but one small example of Nettie's decorating flair.

The next morning, when Nettie and I were all set to go out and do a little shopping, Usher declined to come along. "I'm a little tired," he said. "You two go along. I'll stay in and relax."

Okay, I thought. He'll probably get some reading done.

We returned a few hours later. I expected to find Usher up and dressed, ready to tell me what he did all morning, wanting to hear about what I had done. That's the way it always was with Usher and me.

I walked into the bedroom and found a dying man. It was incredible. Hours before he seemed perfectly fine. Now he was drooping, very, very weak, having great difficulty speaking.

Nettie called her friend Morty. He rushed over and with great difficulty, succeeded in getting Usher into the back seat of his car. We headed to the nearest hospital. I held Usher in my arms; I breathed into his mouth. But I knew he was dying.

"Don't put him in the emergency room. He's dead," I cried when we reached the hospital. They took him from me anyway. They tried whatever they could to save him but to no avail. He died during the night, a Friday night. If God was taking him, I thought, He would choose to take him on the Sabbath.

Five years earlier, Usher had been diagnosed with leukemia, and without his knowledge, I visited his doctor to get the prognosis. He could go five years or more, I was told.

I thought of Dr. Jacoby, one of Usher's congregants who had come to synagogue one day and told him, "Rabbi, you're going to be seeing more of me from now on. I just learned I had leukemia. But I was told I can live for years. So I want to do whatever I can to make that happen."

Ultimately Dr. Jacoby moved to Florida where he lived for more than eighteen years. Now, when the doctor told me Usher had five years or more, my perennial optimism took over. "Oh, Usher's case will be like Dr. Jacoby's; he will live longer than eighteen years."

When the diagnosis was made, Usher had made me promise not to tell anyone, and of course I kept my word. But when he died, I felt regret and guilt over not telling his children. It was such a terrible shock to them. They had no warning. I, on the other hand, had seen the increasing signs, the weight loss, the weakness. During our trips, he always had to check in with doctors to have his blood tested. On our last trip to Jerusalem, I insisted he use a wheelchair in the airport. He was most reluctant but had to give in.

Still, it was a "sudden death" – an expression I had until then only heard in connection with golf. Did leukemia cause his death? I never asked. I never knew. Usher was in his early seventies. But he was a youthful seventies, an alive seventies. He still had a thick head of hair. He still looked so good, always spic-and-span. He still was so vibrant.

Saturday night we were supposed to have dinner at the home of Usher's sister, Ruchel Potack, who also lived in Florida. Although she was older than Usher, he always referred to her as his kid sister, which wasn't altogether incorrect, as she was the youngest girl in the family. When I called with the terrible news, she was thunderstruck. All she could say was, "But what will I do with the dinner?"

In the midst of the shock and dismay, Michael took over. He made all the arrangements. Sunday morning I flew back to New York on the same plane that contained Usher's body. Usher had always wanted his friend Rabbi Yakov Rosenberg, whom he knew from the Seminary, to eulogize him. Michael got in touch with him at his home in Florida and arranged for him to come up to New York.

The funeral was on Monday at the Kew Garden Hills Jewish Center. The crowd was overflowing. Aside from his congregation and other Conservative, Orthodox, Reform, secular, and *Lubavitcher* Jews, even gentile people came out to say goodbye. They spilled out of the sanctuary and the ballroom downstairs onto the streets. Usher was such a beloved figure, and his death was so unexpected.

In addition to Rabbi Rosenberg, Usher's brother, Mordecai, spoke. Rabbi Fabian Schoenfeld, from the big Orthodox synagogue in Kew Garden Hills, who was a distant cousin of mine, spoke. This was most unusual. An Orthodox rabbi, as a rule, will not speak in a Conservative synagogue. But Usher was unusual.

After the services, we followed the hearse with Usher's body, walking down the street past our house. It was a cold, bleak day with intermittent snow and gusty wind. Then those of us who would attend the burial in Jerusalem got into cars and drove to the airport. Because of the bad weather, the plane was delayed.

The time in Israel was a blur. One thing I remember is my grandson Avi, a boy of about eight at the time, sitting alone in a corner of the chapel and reciting psalms. To Avi and the other grandchildren, Usher was the only grandfather they ever knew.

The burial was so strange. The body was laid in the earth, wrapped in a shroud, without a casket. Dust to dust.

We sat *shiva* in Jerusalem for two days and then returned to New York for the remaining days. There was no end to the people who came to pay their respects – from the congregation, from the Seminary, from the political realm, from Kingsborough, from Marine Park, from Port Chester, from the Queens Library Board which Usher was a member of. Among them were people I didn't even know.

The weather was still inclement. When there was a snowstorm the last few days of the *shiva*, I was glad. By this time, I had too much of people and wanted nothing more than to be left alone.

Usher's impact still lingers. Recently a woman approached me at the Park East Synagogue in Manhattan. "I owe what I am today to Usher Kirshblum," she said. "I was having trouble with my husband. My life was so dismal. Rabbi Kirshblum counseled me, guided me, and helped me obtain a *get*. And," she added, "I wasn't even a member of his congregation."

Twenty years after Usher's death, I attended a function at the Kew Garden Hills Jewish Center honoring Judge Moe Weinstein, and was taken aback by the many people who came over to talk to me about Usher. They reminded me how people used to call him "the greatest *mitzvah* factory of all times." He would react to anyone's plight or situation, they recalled. You didn't have to belong to his *shul*, you didn't have to be Conservative, you didn't even have to be Jewish, they said.

Someone mentioned the former cantor of the Kew Garden Hills Jewish Center. He had a beautiful voice but also a terrible gambling problem. He would borrow from people in the synagogue and fail to repay them. Time and again Usher gave him money and never got it back. Ultimately this cantor got in trouble with the Mafia over an unpaid gambling debt. Some very unsavory characters came to his home and threatened his life. Usher met with them and arranged a payment schedule.

How did Usher deal with such people? He had the knack of how to approach them. He had the facility to deal with all kinds of people. And when it came to getting raises, he was always arguing on behalf of the synagogue staff. He was the last one to get a raise.

Together with Dr. Ernest Schwartz, head of the Judaic Department at Queens College, I established the annual Usher Kirshblum Memorial Lecture at Queens College. State Senator Emanuel Gold arranged for the New York State funding for the series. The first lecturer was Isaac Bashevis Singer, who spoke about Yiddish as a living, not a dead language. He was outstanding.

This lecture series, along with the memories of people who knew and loved him, are the legacies of Usher Kirshblum, an extraordinary rabbi and human being, whose life I was so fortunate to share for eleven years.

PART FOUR

Usher and I, c. 1978

At the going-away party for Susan, Arthur and their children before they made *Aliyah*. Eliezer Kirshblum, Usher's son, is playing the accordion. 1981

At Leonard and my wedding. From left to right, Rabbi Saul Teplitz who officiated, Usher's son Eliezer Kirshblum who acted as cantor,and Leonard's sons Michael and David who participated (along with my sons Arthur and Michael) in the ceremony

Leonard's father Dan cuts the challah at our wedding

Leonard and I about to embark on our first cruise, the maiden voyage of the Crown Princess from Southampton, England to New York for *Rosh Hashanah*, 1990

Dancing the night away on a Crystal Cruise

A gathering of the clan at Viegey

Janet and Michael -- they have always
been there for me

With Myrna Katz Frommer who wrote this book with me and her husband Harvey. There was never any doubt about whom I wanted to help me write my memoirs

With longtime friends Rabbi Saul and Mim Teplitz. Saul officiated at my children's wedding as well as at Leonard's and mine. Mim and I worked on many a Women's League program together through the years

Leonard and I with Selma and Morris (Tiny) Weintraub, dear
friends whom we could always count on

My New York family overlooking the old City of Jerusalem,
Nov 1993 – left to right: Michael and Janet, Rachel and Miriam

My Jerusalem granddaughters, left to right:
Debra, Zipporah, Alissa, Abigail, Sara, and Elisheva overlooked
by my Jerusalem (and only) grandson Avi

A growing family poses at the wedding of Rachel and Nimrod Dayan.
Left to right - bottom row: Elisheva, Janet, Miriam, Abigail, Sara, me;
middle row: Susan, Debra, Nimrod, Rachel, Merav (Avi's wife),
Zipporah, Alissa, Leonard;
top row: David Harbarter (Alissa's husband), Michael, Arthur, Avi,
Eyal Haimovsky (Abigail's husband), Micah Avni (Sara's husband)

With Michael (left) and Arthur. How much *naches* they have given me through the years

"Supreme Court, Jerusalem", Painted by Paul Benney 1994

Arthur became imbued with the idea of fulfilling James Rothschild's vision of a Supreme Court Building in Jerusalem. Here he is in a painting with the other principals before a model of the building (seated, far left) along with (seated left to right): Prime Minister Yitzhak Rabin, construction supervisor Eliezer Rahat, philosopher Isaiah Berlin, Supreme Court President Meir Shamear, Lord Rothschild, Mayor of Jerusalem Teddy Kollek; (standing left to right): Foreign Minister Shimon Peres, President Chaim Herzog, Judge Shimon Tzug, architect Ram Karmi; architect Ada Karmi Melamed

Bliss is being kissed by granddaughters Rachel (right)
and Miriam at my 90th birthday party

At the banquet honoring the establishment of the Helen Fried Kirshblum Goldstein Chair of Practical Rabbinics at the Jewish Theological Seminary, from left to right: Vice Chancellor William Lebeau, Rabbinical School Associate Dean Allen Kensky (who occupied the chair), me, Leonard, and Chancellor Ismar Schorsch

Leonard and I with Chancellor Ismar Schorsch. Of all the Seminary chancellors I've known, I've had the closest relationship with Ismar Schorsch. I admire him as a scholar and leader; I also cherish him as a dear friend

Presidents of Women's League at the 2002 Convention.
I'm the one on the far left

XI

INTERMEZZO

I WAS ON MY OWN AGAIN. Teaching at Kingsborough continued to provide me with much satisfaction. Queens Borough President Donald Manes appointed me to Usher's seat on the Queens Library Board, and I came to enjoy that position greatly. I rarely missed a meeting and attended every library convention I could get to.

I had never ceased being active in Women's League, but now I gave leadership-training courses more frequently and pursued board activities more fervently. The Seminary had become my second home. I'd watched it grow over the years into a premier learning institution, respected throughout the academic world, and it was a source of pride and fulfillment for me to be involved in its fund-raising projects. At the same time, I tried to take advantage of the tremendous opportunities it gave me to enhance my knowledge of Judaism through lectures and courses.

My dear friend and mentor Rabbi Heschel died not too long after Usher, and the Mathilde Schechter Award, given to him posthumously, was accepted by his wife. I was so taken by Sylvia Heschel's grace and modesty and thought what a pity it was that we had not gotten to know each other while her husband was alive. Since then, however, we have become very close friends, and I regularly attend the *Yahrtzeit* gathering she holds in her home on the anniversary of Rabbi Heschel's death. A concert pianist of considerable talent, Sylvia comes from a Reform background. She became observant after marrying Rabbi Heschel much as I did after marrying Usher.

We never talked about our widowhood. Still, I expect that although Sylvia's life was full in the years following her husband's death, she missed him terribly. Certainly the loss of Usher left a gaping hole in mine.

And then I came to be disappointed with some of the congregants. When you are the wife of a rabbi, you are treated like the queen of the neighborhood. You think everyone is your friend. To learn this is actually not the case can be an abrupt awakening.

Usher's arrangement with his board was that the house was to be his as long as he lived and wanted to stay in it. He asked the same privilege be extended to me. But even though I was active in the community and a favorite of many, the board members refused, on the grounds that I was Usher's second wife. All they would agree to was that I could live in the house for a few years after he died. It was a decision that pained Usher greatly.

When it came time for me to surrender the house, things became ugly. Some of the board members were curious to know how much Usher had left me. One of them had the chutzpah to call our insurance agent and ask how much life insurance Usher had owned. My agent told him, "If you want that information, ask Mrs. Kirshblum for it." Then this same man went to the insurance office and confronted the agent in person, only to get the same reply.

But I had many loyal friends in Kew Garden Hills, and they rallied to my side. Some of them said to me, "Helen, buy the house. That way you can continue to live here, and no one will be doing you any favors."

I took their advice. I didn't get a bargain by any means, but ultimately it proved to be the right decision, because by the time I was ready to move, real estate values had increased. I sold the house and made a nice little profit.

Michael was furious over the way I was treated. He and Janet were my bulwarks during that time. As I had in the wake of Al's death, I turned to my children for solace and took comfort in reflecting on what decent human beings they were and what successes they had made of their lives.

Taking his father's advice, Arthur began his professional life as an accountant for the Internal Revenue Service. Al Fried had specialized in tax accounting. He knew a lot of people who worked at the IRS and felt it was a good place to begin a career.

One day Susan called me. "Mother, if you're anywhere near a radio at three P.M., you can hear Arthur being interviewed."

"Whatever for?" I asked.

"He was selected as the example of an Internal Revenue Service representative who is kind and wants to help people."

If not for Susan, I'd never have known. Arthur was very much like his father in that way. He didn't want to be fussed over.

While at the IRS, Arthur went to Brooklyn Law School at night. He graduated with honors and passed the bar. But instead of practicing law, he got a job with Merrill Lynch. Before long, he was literally pirated away by Lehman Brothers. At his interview, he made it clear he was an observant Jew who would not be able to be reached from Friday sundown to Saturday sundown and would require kosher food in the company dining room.

He and Susan were such an unusual couple. Once, I happened to be visiting them prior to tax time when they were making out a list of the charities they planned to make donations to in the coming year. They were so young with so much ahead of them, a growing family, and the need for a bigger apartment. And yet giving was already a major consideration in their financial planning.

Ultimately they bought one of those big old wooden houses in Flatbush with a wide porch out front, a nice backyard, and enough room to accommodate a family of six children! There was Alissa, then Sara, then Avi, the only boy, Abigail, Zipporah (Zippy), and Debra.

How did Susan manage? I don't know. She never had any help. She is one of those high-energy people who requires very little sleep and is always on the go. She did everything herself, even baked her own *challah*s and taught the children to bake *challah*s as well. It was a very active household.

Alissa was about to graduate from Flatbush Day School when Arthur and Susan began to make plans to emigrate to Israel. With all the intermarriage they saw about them, they felt Israel was the only place they could feel secure about raising their children in a Jewish environment.

By this time, Arthur was the managing partner of Lehman Brothers. The people there were distraught at the prospect of his leaving. They made him fabulous offers, hoping he'd change his mind. But he had already gotten the wheels in motion by returning to college at night to study hospital administration.

While the hospitals in Israel were good, their administration was poor; directorships were usually filled by retired military figures. Arthur felt this would be an area where he could make a contribution to Israeli society, so he completed his studies and went to Israel to interview at various hospitals.

All the interviews went very well, and he came back home fully expecting to receive offers. But he heard from no one. It was very disappointing, and at this point he felt that if a job was not forthcoming, they would not make the move. "Mother, I have enough money for the family to live comfortably for the rest of our lives," he told me. "But I don't want to move to Israel unless I can do something purposeful there."

Then, from out of the blue, he received a phone call from Boston. "My name is Moe Feurstein," the caller said to Arthur. "You don't know me, but I have heard about you from some people I know in New York, and I have a proposition that may be of interest to you." He explained that a good friend of his was leaving his position as director of the Rothschild Foundation, and they were looking for a replacement. Would he be interested?

Arthur was interviewed by Lady Dorothy Rothschild in London. She was so pleased with him, she wanted him to begin immediately. But Arthur said he must first go home and speak to his family. Soon after, he got back to Lady Rothschild telling her that he would be happy to accept. She said to him, "Write us a memo of what you would expect from us."

He listed three requirements: an office in Jerusalem, the education of all his children for as long as they wish to attend school, and a salary based on the cost of living index in Israel. Lady Rothschild responded, "Your list sounds very meager, but if it is what you want, we are happy to provide it for you."

That was it. Usher and I threw a great big farewell party for the family. It was a joyous occasion. But my happiness was tinged with regret. Not only would they be so far away, their primary language would become Hebrew. I had never learned to speak or read Hebrew. I could barely get through the *siddur*. Naturally they all became bilingual, and the children flow in and out of Hebrew, especially when they don't want me to know what they're talking about, much in the way my parents would flow in and out of Polish when they wanted to keep something from me.

In Jerusalem, Arthur and Susan bought two ground-floor apartments in a building on Balfour Street, a short distance from the Prime Minister's residence. One had been the office of a religious women's organization, the other of an insurance company. They broke through to make one large apartment for the family.

Shortly after they made *aliyah*, Susan got pregnant again. They brought the baby girl to *shul* the first *Shabbat* after she was born and named her Elisheva, *Eli* for "my God" and *sheva* for "seven." She was their seventh gift from God.

By then, Elisheva's five sisters and her one brother had made an adjustment to their new home. For Alissa it was easy because she had belonged to a youth organization in Brooklyn. But even Zippy, who used to cry, "I'll never speak that language – I hate it," got over that feeling quickly.

Whenever I would visit and speak of home, meaning America, they would open their eyes wide and say, "But Nanny, *this* is home."

No sooner would I walk in the front door, they would all come running. They loved to rummage through my suitcase and try on my gowns, hats, and especially my high-heeled shoes. And if they messed things up a bit, I couldn't care less.

Of course, I never failed to arrive without gifts for them all, and more than once was touched to realize how much they were appreciated. The summer after Usher died, I was walking with twelve-year-old Abigail down King George Street and passed a shop window with antique jewelry. A pin in the shape of a butterfly with a diamond suspended on the bottom caught my eye. We went inside to check it out. But when I heard it was more than a thousand dollars, I backed off.

On the way back home, Abigail tugged at my hand. "You know, Nanny, you're very funny," she said. "You bring us so many presents whenever you come. Why don't you buy a present for yourself for a change?"

"Well," I told her, "I work very hard for my money. And I don't really need that pin."

"But we don't really need the things you buy us either," she said.

I thought about it. The next day I went back to the shop and I bought that pin. And every time I wear it, I think of Abigail.

Whenever my teaching schedule allowed, I would try to get to Jerusalem to celebrate *Purim* with the family. They would hold a gala *seudah* in their home following the reading of the *Megillah* in synagogue. Friends who had made *aliyah* from Brooklyn around the same time as they did were invited. For weeks before, everyone planned and worked on his or her costume. Each year meant a new costume with everyone trying to outdo one another, each costume more fantastic than the next and kept secret until the night of *Purim*. Only Arthur wore the same tuxedo and top hat year after year. But it was the one night of the year when we had the opportunity to see the otherwise dignified paterfamilias get a little tipsy.

The Rothschild Foundation had offices in Jerusalem, London, and Geneva. In the summers, Arthur would rent a house in Geneva so the family could be together when the children were out of school.

One summer, I was visiting them in Geneva, and I happened to spend some time alone with Zippy, who was about ten years old at the time. Zippy was the free spirit of the bunch; she marched to her own drummer. The others used to tease her because she didn't quite fit in. And there were times when she seemed a little awkward.

This day we were sitting together in the living room. No one else was around, which was just the way I wanted it. I felt it was so important to have private time with each of the children. Now, we suddenly noticed a peacock strutting about in the garden. "Let's go out and take a closer look," I said to her.

So Zippy and I walked out gingerly, being careful not to frighten the peacock away. He saw us, stopped, and before our eyes spread out his plumage. It was magnificent, a gigantic arc with turquoise circles in the feathers. "Look, Zippy," I said to her, "see how the peacock shows himself to us. How proud he is. Look how he keeps his head up high, not buried in his feathers."

We began talking about how one should walk and talk, how important it is to present oneself with aplomb. After that, I noticed Zippy began paying attention to her image. The teacher in me, never at rest, had used the peacock as a model for teaching an awkward little girl, who has since turned into a most graceful young woman.

Ultimately Arthur decided to buy a house in Geneva. Then he learned that you can't buy property in Switzerland unless you are a citizen. So instead he found a magnificent mansion in Viegy, France, adjoining the Swiss border. It came with a second building, formerly servants' quarters, which Arthur turned into offices. The Manor, as it's called, is a tremendous house, with a gorgeous swimming pool. But a family with seven children has always managed to fill it up. And it's always been a welcoming home to family and friends.

The same can be said of the Frieds' Jerusalem home. At one time I was asked whether Susan would be willing to host a group of Women's League delegates for a *Shabbat* afternoon meeting. Of course she was.

But when I arrived a half hour before the scheduled time, it looked as if nothing was happening. I was so surprised. Although I hadn't asked Susan to prepare anything, I was certain she understood.

Of course she had. Within ten minutes, the huge dining room table was filled with all kinds of cakes and strudels, all of which she had baked herself, bowls of fruit, and dishes filled with nuts and sweets. It was a beautiful and inviting setting.

Arthur had said to me in a wisecracking way, "What are the ladies going to do here? Look at the house, ooh and ahh at the kids?"

But to my amazement, when the program got underway and a cantor who had accompanied the group sang, Arthur indicated to me that he would like to speak. He welcomed the delegates and delivered a nice little talk based on that week's *Torah* portion.

Of all of Arthur's achievements as director of the Rothschild Foundation, I think his work in connection with the Supreme Court building ranks supreme. Its erection was the realization of the dream of James Rothschild who, like his father, Edmond, was greatly instrumental in the creation of the Jewish state.

James Rothschild had envisioned Israel's house of parliament and Supreme Court building standing one beside the other, and he had offered the funds for both. But only the *Knesset* was built. David Ben-Gurion wanted the Supreme Court building to be located on Mount Scopus. Somehow that never happened, and through the years, the Supreme Court continued to meet in an old building in the Russian Compound of Jerusalem.

After James died in 1967, Dorothy Rothschild took over the running of the Rothschild Foundation. She revived the idea of building the Supreme Court building beside the *Knesset* to mark the one hundredth anniversary of her father-in-law's connection to Israel. By this time, Yitzhak Shamir was prime minister. Unlike Ben-Gurion, he said, "If you're going to donate the money, you can build it beside the *Knesset*."

Arthur became imbued with the idea of fulfilling James Rothschild's vision. He had always been bothered by the fact that the distinguished judges did not even have an adequate restroom in the building in which they met. He took over the project, overseeing its design, construction, and decoration, down to the very last detail. From an international competition of architects, an Israeli brother and sister team were selected, but not before an exhibition of models from throughout the world were displayed in an exhibition at the Israel Museum. When the building was completed, it received rave reviews from critics like Paul Goldberger of the *New York Times*.

A huge oil painting that for some reason has always reminded me of the famous picture of the signers of the Declaration of Independence, hangs in the vestibule of this magnificent Supreme Court building. Around a table displaying the model are a group of men, some seated, others standing and looking down. Among them are Yitzhak Rabin, Shimon Peres, two justices of the Supreme Court, Teddy Kollek, and Arthur. The pair of architects are pictured as well; they are the only ones not in dark jackets or judicial robes.

Arthur is a hard act to follow. But Michael has managed to do just that. I used to think that he tended to imitate his older brother. Like Arthur, Michael went to Brooklyn Law School. Like Arthur, Michael became Modern Orthodox. After Arthur bought a great house in Viegy, Michael built a big, beautiful house in Copake, near the golf course. And like his brother, Michael ended up doing very well financially.

In his first position, as the director of the financial aid department at Manhattan Community College, Michael was so successful that Newark Community College lured him away with a much better deal. But it turned out to be an unhappy change. In Manhattan, he was very close to the minority students. In Newark, where he was the only white person and the only Jew, he found himself being resented as an outsider and newcomer.

The unpleasant situation at work prompted him to go to Brooklyn Law School at night, where he outdid his brother, graduating first in his class. Michael not only contributed to the *Law Review*, he was one of its editors and wrote an opinion that was cited by the Second Court of Appeals. It is interesting how all through elementary school, high school, and even in college, neither Arthur nor Michael were extraordinary students. It was only in law school that they really began to apply their gifts.

After he graduated and passed the bar, Michael applied for a job at Proskauer and Rose, a prominent Jewish law firm. His interview went very well, but the message he received was that the firm generally hires graduates of Ivy League law schools.

"Michael," I said when he told me what happened, "you have offers from other prestigious firms. Why don't you get in touch with Proskauer and tell them you have these other offers. Tell them you have to make a decision, but your heart is with them. And tell them why."

He listened to me, and they hired him.

Michael was at Proskauer and Rose for about five years, on his way to becoming a partner, when he realized he wanted to try something else. He got a job with Related Company, an up-and-coming real estate development firm that built apartment houses, office buildings, and malls. Ultimately Michael became president of the financial component of Related. Then he decided he'd like to go off on his own and in 1999 began Phoenix Realty, which today has offices in New York and Los Angeles.

He's also a restaurateur. Around the time Phoenix Realty was started, Michael and his friend and partner Alan Hermes opened Shallots, a gourmet kosher restaurant in the Sony building atrium on Madison Avenue. Michael has always had a feel for the culinary arts. He was the only one in the family who could carve a turkey with flair and aplomb. He was the only one who picked up recipes from me and tried them out on his own. And he always had a healthy appetite to accompany his love of good food.

When I went to Shallots for the first time, when I took in the elegant David Rockwell interior, sat down in one of the plush booths, and looked over a menu with such sophisticated dishes as lamb tagine, duck confit, and gnocchi in a pesto sauce, I could not help but think back to the time Al Fried was dying and Michael made a traditional *Shabbat* dinner for me. And I understood the line from the twenty-third psalm: "My cup runneth over."

Janet is the perfect partner for Michael. She shares his ambition. Early on in their marriage she worked because she had to. Now she continues to work, but it is for the benefit of others. She is the program director for the Teen Tutor Reading Partner Program, which trains teenagers in the New York City schools to become tutors for children who have difficulty learning to read.

Janet's ambition extends to her expectations for her daughters. Rachel and Miriam were not extraordinary students, yet they attended and graduated from Ramaz, the elite Orthodox day school in Manhattan – with no small amount of help from their mother. Like their father, Rachel and Miriam did not hit their stride scholastically in elementary or high school.

They had a good time in Ramaz anyway, where they were involved in many activities and had busy social lives. Still, when Rachel graduated from high school, I said to Janet, "This diploma belongs to you as much as Rachel."

When Alissa graduated from high school, I decided to give her an unusual gift: a trip to the destination of her choice. She picked Paris, the French Riviera, and London, so we worked out an itinerary that began in Paris, then went on to Nice, and ended up in London. She had a steady boyfriend at the time. But when I asked whether she'd mind leaving him, she was nonchalant. "He'll be here when I come back," she said.

That turned out not to be the case. Still I'm certain Alissa had no regrets about spending the summer with her Nanny. In Paris she had the opportunity to meet Al Fried's family and to learn the stories of their lives, particularly what happened to them during the Second World War.

Denise, one of the cousins, owned a factory that manufactured high fashion women's clothing. The family took us there and were most generous to us. Nearly twenty years later, I still have a suit they gave me, which is as fashionable today as it was then.

Alissa and I spent hours wandering through the streets of the Left Bank, looking in store windows, stopping for café au lait and glacé at outdoor cafés and watching the crowds go by. Our hours were blissful, except for the time we were walking down the Boulevard Saint-Germain des Prés, when she suddenly stopped and grabbed my arm. "Nanny, look," she cried in alarm pointing at a group of boys coming our way. "They're Arabs. Let's cross the street."

I was so surprised. Living in Jerusalem, Alissa was among Arabs all the time. I knew Susan and Arthur raised their children to be tolerant, not to judge others on their religion, race, or ethnicity. Many were the times I had seen Susan giving money to Arabs, who came to her door collecting for one charity or another.

"Don't be silly," I said to Alissa. "They're not going to bother you."

We didn't cross the street. The boys passed us innocently and continued on their way. But I wondered about it afterwards. Why was this young Israeli girl so frightened? Why was there such mistrust? And if it existed on her side, it must exist on the other side as well. I had witnessed a small example of what would become an increasingly worse situation, because mistrust between Arab and Jew is far deeper today.

Alissa loved Paris so much, she prevailed upon me to extend our stay. But in revising our itinerary, we were unable to get another flight to Nice and had to go down to the Riviera by train instead. We did manage to get a flight from Nice to London, but with our changed dates, I had to change hotels in London, which wasn't easy at the height of the tourist season. When we walked into the East End hotel, where I'd reserved a room, and saw a bunch of punk kids with purple hair behind the front desk, I knew this was not the place for us. It was just before *Shabbat*, and we had to get settled. I hailed a cab and asked the taxi driver to take us to one of the more expensive hotels.

With all our little adventures and misadventures, it was a great trip, and after we returned to Jerusalem, I told the other children Alissa's gift vacation would be the first of a tradition. Every summer I would take a different grandchild on a trip to wherever he or she would like to go. As things turned out, I would do a lot of traveling in the years to come, but not with them.

XII

A GENTLE PASTOR

AFTER BRINGING ALISSA BACK HOME, I spent about a week in Jerusalem with the family and then returned to Kew Garden Hills. It was early September. School would not begin for a few weeks, but one morning I decided I'd go down to the college anyway and get myself set for the coming semester.

I was just about to leave when the phone rang. It was a friend from Women's League calling to bring me up to date on all the news. We chatted for a while. Before I hung up, I mentioned I would be in her neighborhood that afternoon. She lived in Manhattan Beach and was a congregant at Temple Beth El. It was then she told me her rabbi's wife had died a few months ago. The poor woman had been ill for over a year, she said. The rabbi had been very devoted to her, and had cared for her until the end.

Later that day, I telephoned Rabbi Leonard Goldstein from my office in Kingsborough and expressed my condolences. I knew Jeanette casually, I said, and had thought her a lovely, very attractive woman.

He thanked me for calling. Then he told me he was retiring from Temple Beth El and in the process of selling his house. "The best thing the synagogue could have done for me when they hired me was not give me a house," he said. "I had to buy one, and now I'm selling it at a substantial profit. As a matter of fact, I'm just about to leave for Manhattan, where I'm looking for an apartment."

"Oh," I said impulsively, "will you be driving into the city?"

"Yes, I am."

"Would it be all right if I parked my car in your driveway and hopped a ride with you?" I asked. "I'm planning to visit my daughter-in-law in Peter Cooper Village, but would just as soon not drive into Manhattan."

"Of course," he said.

So I drove over to his house, parked my car in his driveway, and we went into Manhattan together in his car. I never gave a thought as to how I'd get back.

Over the years I had seen Leonard around at various conferences and conventions. We knew many of the same people and were familiar with the latest issues confronting Conservative Judaism. So on the ride in, we had plenty to talk about. At the same time, I was recalling a brief encounter we had in Geneva some thirty years earlier.

It was the last day of the World Council of Synagogues conference. I was running down the stairs of the hotel when a gentleman stopped me. At first I couldn't place him. Then I realized he was Leonard Goldstein, the rabbi of a synagogue in New London, Connecticut, where one of my Women's League friends was a congregant.

"Where are you going in such a hurry?" he asked.

"I'm headed into town to buy a gift for my mother," I said. Then I added, "Why don't you come along?"

He did and helped me pick out a handsome clock. The chore was accomplished so quickly, we had enough time to stop for coffee at an outdoor café. Then we returned to the hotel and went our separate ways.

One evening some years later, after Leonard had left New London to become rabbi of Temple Beth El in Manhattan Beach, I was delivering a lecture at that synagogue on the role of women in Judaism. I was married to Usher at the time, and the thrust of my comments reflected his conservative viewpoint. During my talk, I noticed Leonard standing in the corner at the rear of the hall. Afterwards we exchanged pleasantries. He was very polite. But, of course, he didn't agree with a word I said.

Now, strangely, life had thrown us together once again. Leonard dropped me off in Peter Cooper Village but not before offering to give me a lift back to Manhattan Beach. I spent some hours with Janet and Rachel. Michael came home; we all had dinner. Then, as promised, Leonard picked me up and drove me back to his house and my car.

A few days later, he telephoned. Once he called me, I knew I could call him, and I did not wait for him to call. We began to see each other with some regularity. I helped him move, suggesting what items he should keep and what to sell. Things progressed swiftly.

Leonard had rented a one-bedroom apartment on East Seventy-ninth Street. One day, while I was in his apartment, I pulled a muscle in my back. To this day, my remedy for back pain is to lie on the floor in a fetal position, with my knees close to my chest until the pain subsides. That was where I was, half asleep, when I felt a slight tap on my shoulder. I opened my eyes and dangling before me was a beautiful gold-braid bracelet set with dark sapphires. "This is your engagement present if you will marry me," Leonard said.

I felt Leonard was right for me. He wasn't short. He wasn't really tall, but tall enough. He was worldly and informed. He was nice looking and exceedingly kind.

Usher used to kibitz me. "Helen, after I go, you can't have a five-year plan any more. You'll have to make it shorter." It was now three and a half years since he died, and just as I had felt in the wake of Al Fried's death, I knew I did not belong in a single world. I reached out for the bracelet, put it on, and have not taken it off since.

Before we began seeing each other, I had no idea Leonard was eleven years younger than I was, and when I first learned his age, I refrained from telling him mine. But ultimately I told him how old I was, and I told him about my denture. By the time we got married, he knew everything about me except that I had had an abortion. No one but Al Fried ever knew about that.

Leonard and I realized we couldn't live in his little one-bedroom apartment, and we began looking around for another place. We pooled our money hoping to find a two-bedroom apartment on the East Side. But nothing we saw in our price range appealed to us. Then we found an apartment on East Seventy-second Street that seemed perfect. The price was a great deal more than we planned on spending. We talked it over. Real estate had proved to be a good investment for both of us in the past. We bought the apartment and have never had a moment's regret.

Before I left the house in Kew Garden Hills, I had the biggest tag sale in the world. At 7:00 in the morning, people were lined up all the way down the street. I got rid of a lot of stuff. Only the things I loved best came along with me to my new home. One thing was missing, however – the baby grand piano I had bought in installments with Mama back when I was a girl. It took a while to retrieve, but ultimately the piano found its way to my Manhattan apartment.

I had given the baby grand to Michael and Janet when I married Usher because there already was a piano in his living room that fit in perfectly. After a while, they redecorated their apartment, had no room for it and gave it to a friend.

I was living in Manhattan for a while when their friend called one day. "I'm moving out of my house," she told me. "What do you want me to do with the piano?"

Leonard and I drove up to her home in Scarsdale to find my beautiful baby grand was a mess. There were cigarette burns in the fine wood finish and missing ivories on the keyboard. Still, I was determined to take it back.

"We'll have it redone," I said. We had the piano picked up and brought to a place for refurbishment. Today it has a place of honor in my living room, and though I hardly play any longer, its presence gives me great pleasure.

At first I was reluctant to move to Manhattan. I thought I knew Manhattan, and it didn't seem right for me. But as I discovered, I didn't know Manhattan very well at all. The Upper East Side, with all the art museums and galleries, restaurants and theaters, and places of particular Jewish interest like the Jewish Museum so close by, has turned out to be a great place to live.

Our wedding, a gift from Arthur and Michael, was at the Water's Edge in Long Island City. This time the sun shone brightly, and the view of the East River, with the Queensborough Bridge and New York City skyline in the distance, was dazzling. Our dear friend Saul Teplitz married us. Arthur and Michael, as well as Leonard's two sons, Michael and David, participated in the ceremony. Usher's son, Eliezer, acted as cantor, and in a beautiful toast afterwards, he reflected on Usher's and my marriage, which moved and honored me greatly. Eliezer had accepted me from the start, and it was a source of joy to know he continued to care about me and my happiness, even to the point of celebrating my marriage to a man who was taking a place once held by his beloved father.

On the other hand, it was a source of pain to see how my grandchildren could not accept Leonard. They seemed to resent him, and this attitude persisted for years. Usher was the only grandfather they ever knew.

Ironically, none of them ever got to know the grandfather I wanted them to have most. Al Fried was the role model I envisioned, a modern, American grandfather.

Even my children, though they were generous and welcoming, held back from Leonard for a long while. Why don't they give him a chance, I would think. Leonard is so loveable, so kind, so good to children. Ultimately time solved the problem, and everyone came to appreciate Leonard for the wonderful person he is. But there was that period of adjustment.

Marrying Leonard was an easy adjustment for me. He was far more liberal in observance and outlook than Usher, and, if truth be told, Leonard's positions were far closer to my own. I now felt free to articulate my heartfelt views, especially on the role of women. I do believe that women should be counted towards a *minyan* and receive *aliyot*, that there should be women rabbis and cantors. Still, out of loyalty to Usher's memory, I will never accept an *aliyah* myself.

Although Leonard appears to be gentle, he can be quite firm. I think he was even more assertive with his board than Usher. During the period when there was a great deal of debate over the question of liberalizing the role of women in the synagogue, fewer than ten men showed up for *mincha* services on the first day of *Rosh Hashanah*. He decided he would hold the service anyway, counting the women who were there to make up the *minyan*.

After the holidays, when the board reconvened and began to resume the debate, Leonard told them, "There's no need to discuss the matter any further. There may be a de jure question in your minds, but de facto, it has already happened. From now on, women will be counted towards a *minyan*."

Leonard was an outstanding pastor, sympathetic and compassionate. His concern has always been more with people than delivering sermons. He does not consider himself an orator. But every time I heard him speak, I thought he was outstanding. His demeanor is warm and genuine; he has a great sense of justice. And unlike most of the rabbis I know, he has very little ego. He doesn't become friendly with a person because he is a somebody. Leonard's approach is to get to know you as you are, regardless of your status. It's your character that matters to him.

His modesty belies his accomplishments. It was only by accident that I learned Leonard had majored in Latin and classical Greek at Yeshiva

University where he graduated cum laude. At the same time, he is drawn to sports as much as the classics. I think the fact that he was such an ardent football fan led to his decision in 1948 to begin his rabbinical career at the only synagogue in Green Bay, Wisconsin.

Leonard's background was very different from mine and from my first two husbands. His parents were American-born. He grew up in an upper-middle-class environment in Trenton, New Jersey, where his father was in the insurance business. In addition to Mitzi, his natural sister, he had an adopted sister, Frances, or Buddy as she was called, a Polish girl who came to work for Leonard's mother when she was about thirteen. She grew very attached to the family, and they to her. Ultimately she converted to Judaism, and Leonard's parents adopted her.

Buddy was a good sport, wonderful with the kids, never jealous of anyone. And she had a very persuasive personality. When Leonard's father was about to turn ninety-five, we decided to make him a birthday party. But "Dapper Dan," as Dan Goldstein was known because he cut such a dashing figure, wouldn't hear of it. He was a widower by then, living at the Sherry Frontenac, one of the last of the grand Jewish hotels in Miami Beach and he was a favorite of the ladies there. "I'm not going to let the women know I'm ninety-five!" he declared.

We argued to no avail. Finally we complained to Buddy. "What's the matter with you?" she said to Leonard's father. She would brook no argument. Finally, Dan relented. It was a marvelous party. A big poster of Dan Goldstein in his First World War uniform set the appropriate mood, and everyone had a grand time.

But we did have to compromise on one thing. The party was advertised as "Dapper Dan's" ninetieth. He told us that none of his lady friends would drive him around any more if they knew how old he really was.

It was Leonard's maternal grandfather, Joseph Finn, who imbued in him a love of *Yiddishkeit* on the one hand and Zionism on the other. Joseph Finn had invested in what was to become Bank Leumi when it first began in the early 1900s. It was not so much a business investment as a commitment to Zionism. Leonard internalized that commitment, and it remained part of his identity all his life.

Evidently his older son inherited his father's Zionistic leanings, because after graduating from Columbia University, Michael made *aliyah*.

For many years, he held the position of director of events for the Israel Museum.

Michael's first wife was very artistic and made us an exquisite *ketubah*, which Michael brought to New York a few weeks before our wedding. Leonard read it over and discovered she had copied the entire text in Hebrew, including the phrase which describes the bride as a virgin. Luckily, a friend of mine was going to Israel just at that time. She took the *ketubah* along with her, had it corrected, and brought it back to us in time for the wedding.

Leonard's younger son, David, was also a Zionist. During the Six-Day War, he left college to work on a *kibbutz*. David was a Ph.D. candidate in neuro-psychology at Yeshiva University, when suddenly he developed a brain tumor that became so severe he ultimately had to leave school. Then for a while, it seemed to be under control. He married. His son, Jonah, was born.

But the problem resurfaced, and his condition worsened. His wife divorced him when he needed her most. We didn't blame her, and we did. I don't know what anyone would have done under the circumstances.

After he suffered a number of strokes, David had to be put into a long-term care facility. It was very painful for Leonard. I have had many experiences of *bikkur cholim* in my life, but never was it more deeply felt than at this terrible time.

In 2001, David died. I shared Leonard's grief with all my heart, knowing there is no worse fate for a parent than to lose a child.

As in my times of loss, Leonard kept himself going by involving himself in many activities. One of his favorite causes has become Open University, the largest university in Israel. This is a school with over thirty thousand students and not one classroom. Students take courses via computers and television. It's a totally twenty-first-century, state-of-the art operation that other universities have come to study and emulate. Anyone, regardless of previous academic achievement, can attend: soldiers, older people, women who didn't get the education they wanted earlier in their lives, new immigrants. Many go on to excellent graduate schools and have successful professional lives.

The Rothschild Foundation was instrumental in getting this institution off the ground, and for a while Arthur served as the International President

of the Friends of Open University. At one point, Arthur was unable to attend one of its New York functions, and his tickets were offered to us. We
went, learned what it was all about, and we have been active in supporting
it ever since, becoming founders and serving on the board of trustees.

Being married to Leonard did not lessen my involvement in organizational life. I even continued giving public speaking courses at Kingsborough
as an adjunct (I had retired from my full time position years before), only
now I was driving from Manhattan into Brooklyn. I was a teaching junkie.
I didn't want to give it up.

Throughout the years I had given many a private course and handed
out many an impromptu tip. It seemed as soon as anyone I met in public
life learned I taught public speaking, he or she wanted some advice. At one
of the national conventions, I was on the dais with the Israeli Minister of
Tourism. True to form he asked if we could get together after the meeting
so I could give him a couple of pointers. I readily agreed and during his
speech I made some mental notes about what he could do to improve his
delivery.

Afterwards I was walking off the dais together with a group of women
when he interrupted me. "Where can we do it?" he asked impatiently.

"Well," I said, "I'll have to find a place."

"But where, oh where?" he persisted.

Heads began to turn. And for the rest of that conference, I continued
to get some pretty curious looks.

One day at the Seminary, I got into a conversation with Vice Chancellor William Lebeau. He thought the Seminary's graduating students could
use a course in public speaking, and I readily agreed. I even agreed to give
one without compensation.

I drew up a syllabus for a course entitled Speech Preparation and
Presence, and Rabbi Lebeau found a place for it in the course schedule. But
not without difficulty. There is always such a great deal of politicking going
on, and I could understand that some of the professors might think a new
course could interfere with their registration. They also, undoubtedly, felt
such a course was not as important as their content courses. Still, we tried
it out, and it was so successful that the powers-that-be decided to continue
it on a once-a-year basis.

What I did was get the students up on their feet as soon as possible,
having them deliver a *d'var Torah*. I videotaped each presentation and

would show it to the class. First another student would assess the talk. Then the student himself or herself would do so. Finally, I would evaluate it. The course had nothing to do with content; that was homiletics. My focus was solely on presentation of one's self, both orally and physically.

It was very difficult. I had no one helping me. I had to operate the video camera and do the teaching. How I handled it, I just don't know. But it worked very well. By this time I had had so much experience in teaching and practicing public speaking, I really knew what I was doing.

Midway through my first semester, Rabbi Lebeau came over to me. "Helen, your teaching without getting paid is very unfair," he said. "I'm putting you on the payroll." That was okay, but it really didn't matter. I was still smitten with teaching, and I would have done it just for the love of it. Two of the many donations I have made to the Seminary are in honor of my students. They symbolize the feeling that has accompanied me during my many decades of teaching – my students give me as much as I give them.

The course continued for about seven years. Afterwards a professional organization was hired to continue providing this type of instruction. It was very expensive, so they got a donor to pay for it. For my part, I was gratified there was an awareness at the Seminary that future rabbis need training in public speaking. No matter how excellent the content of a speech may be, if it is not delivered well, it might as well not have been delivered at all.

One of the reasons I ultimately stopped teaching at both Kingsborough and the Seminary was that I was on the road – or should I say the sea – so often. Leonard loved to travel, and before I met him, while he was still at Temple Beth El and contemplating retirement, he thought about affiliating himself with some kind of travel agency or airline.

At one point, he wrote to many overseas airlines offering himself as a consultant to market Jewish-related trips. The only one who responded was Lufthansa. They wanted to promote Jewish trips to Germany and recommended him to a travel agency. After he retired, Leonard became this agency's consultant on Jewish travel.

At a Rabbinical Assembly convention, he met a rabbi who told him about an agent who booked rabbis for cruises. Leonard followed up on it, and that led to our maiden voyage on the maiden voyage of the *Crown Princess* from Southampton, England, to New York, for *Rosh Hashanah* 1990.

I was reluctant to go. When I was a young woman, my cousins in Port Chester invited Al Fried and me to go out with them on their fishing boat.

We were not on the water for a half hour when I threw up. I vowed never to go on another boat.

Years later, Usher convinced me to give the sea a second try. He booked last-minute reservations on a Greek ship for a tour of the Greek islands. Our accommodations were dreadful. The ship was ugly. I felt seasick all the time and couldn't wait until it was over.

Afterwards I vowed never again. And, I said to myself, this time I really mean it. Yet somehow Leonard had persuaded me to walk the gangplank once more. Only now I had a patch behind my ear that the doctor said was guaranteed to prevent seasickness.

We flew to Southampton. The ship was gorgeous. I thought I was fine. But, as Leonard later told me, the first day we were out I began acting strangely and had difficulty going up and down the stairs. The second day out, he woke up in the middle of the night to find me walking around. When he asked what I was doing, I told him I was throwing out the garbage. Then I said we'd have to change our stateroom because there were squirrels in the walls.

One of the people at our table was a doctor. "Is she wearing a patch?" the doctor asked when Leonard mentioned my weird behavior. "Remove it immediately. It causes hallucinations."

Without the patch, I was back to my old – and this time not seasick – self and free to enjoy a luxurious mode of travel, which in subsequent years would bring me to ports in distant parts of the world and introduce me to a range of extraordinary people.

Leonard and I met Pablo Mané, the impressionist painter from Barcelona, on that maiden voyage. Although his parents were Jewish, Pablo had had no experience with Jewish life whatsoever. He was born in South America, the son of a diplomat, and was a lawyer before he moved to Spain and took up painting. All alone on the cruise, he wandered into the *Rosh Hashanah* service Leonard was conducting and encountered his Jewishness for the first time. It left a lasting impression. Since then, we have visited him in Barcelona, and he has visited us in New York. We even arranged an exhibition of his work at a Manhattan gallery.

After our first cruise, Leonard began accepting assignments two, even three times a year on the Princess line. They always coincided with a Jewish holiday, and Leonard's responsibility was to conduct holiday and Sabbath services.

I found myself getting involved in the marriage reaffirmation ceremonies, which are popular among the older travelers. Traditionally they are done by the ship's captain. But Leonard started performing them for Jewish couples, adapting the ceremony according to the couple's desires. The ship would print up invitations. There would be a reception afterwards. It was a way for the ship to make money, but also it added a significant aspect to many a couple's holiday.

Then Leonard learned that Crystal Cruises was the ultimate in luxury cruises. He called them just around the time that he signed on for a cruise with the Seabourne line and was told they'd decide whether to hire him based on what Seabourne had to say about him.

Seabourne was a small ship with room for only 150 people. But it was very luxurious. Every accommodation was a suite. The price was one thousand dollars a day per person, and the crowd was elite. We became quite friendly with William Hammerstein, the son of Oscar Hammerstein II, who cruised with Seabourne regularly.

The television journalists Howard K. Smith, Bernard Kalb, and Edwin R. Newman were lecturers on board. I was so delighted that they sat at our table, because it gave me the chance to talk to Edwin R. Newman, whose book I had used often in my classes. We met many celebrities aboard ship, and all were exceedingly warm and approachable, with the exception of Barbara Walters. She came with her own group and chose not to mix with anyone else.

The Seabourne cruise lasted three weeks. We traveled through the archipelago of Indonesia and Southeast Asia, stopping at various ports. Before we arrived at Bali, a documentary film producer spoke to the passengers about its history and culture. "You may come to Bali without a religion," he said, "but you will not be able to leave without one."

It was true. The Balinese are Hindus, and everything they do revolves around their faith. Every house has an altar with an offering. We visited a temple in a gorgeous flower-filled outdoor setting with three pools, one for the men, one for the women (like a *mikveh*, where women go after menstruation), and one for the children, who were happily splashing about. We could not help but be taken in by the warmth and spirituality of the place.

Bali was closer to paradise than anyplace I could ever imagine. The scenery was beautiful, the art was beautiful, and the people were beautiful, always smiling, always welcoming. How ironic and dreadful that such a land would become the site of terrorism.

After seeing Bali, I found it difficult to get back on the ship, but when we reached Komodo Island, Leonard could not convince me to get off the ship. This is the only place in the world where the Komodo dragons, twenty-foot-long reptiles, are found. Leonard and the other passengers brave enough to join the native guides were led single file through the island to the place where the man-eating reptiles live. The guides put the people in a cage, and the dragons circled the cage, looking them over. I have always been a most curious person. But this was one adventure I felt I could live without.

The people at Seabourne must have had good things to say about Leonard because after our return, Crystal Cruises hired him for their D-Day Anniversary Cruise in 1994. Since then, we have continued to cruise with Crystal. It is a much bigger line. The full compliment could be as many as nine hundred people. There is so much to do, every facility imaginable, lectures, concerts, theatrical productions, and lavish shows performed by well-known and accomplished artists.

One Friday night after services we were nearing Venice when a young couple from California approached Leonard. "Rabbi, would you marry us?" they asked.

"Are you Jewish?"

They were.

"Well," Leonard said, "I'll be pleased to marry you, but if you don't have a license, you will have to have a civil ceremony when you return home to satisfy state law."

"That's no problem."

He asked whether they wanted to be married on deck or in a stateroom.

"Neither," they said. "We want to get married in Venice beside one of the canals."

Fortunately Leonard knew the chief rabbi of Venice, and when the ship docked, he went to his home and was able to get a *ketubah*. Then Leonard and I, and the bride and groom looked around for a suitable place. We found a lovely park not far from where the ship was docked. It was right beside a canal.

The couple invited some of the people on the cruise. Leonard used his *tallit* as a *chuppah* and performed the ceremony. Afterwards a reception was held on board. It was a unique and beautiful wedding. Today the couple have two children and still keep in touch with us.

We were about to leave on one of the Crystal cruises when I got a call from Lucerne. It was my old friend Eva Wiener, whose husband had died a few years before, with some good news – she was going to get on board and join us when our ship docked in Rome.

Crystal always had a coterie of about six gentlemen to act as dancing partners for unaccompanied women. When I suggested to Eva that she approach one of them, she demurred. "Oh, I wouldn't do a thing like that."

So I looked them over and decided which one I would like to dance with if I wasn't with my husband. "You've got to do me a favor," I said to him. "We're seated at table number four. Come over and let me introduce you to my friend as someone I know. Don't tell her you're an escort."

Well, he did just that. After some conversation, he asked Eva to dance. And she ended up dancing throughout that whole cruise. Ultimately she did discover her dancing partner was an escort. But by that time it didn't matter, because she knew him as a person.

We took two world cruises on the *Crystal Symphony*. They began in Los Angeles right after New Year's and ended in England three months later. One went to Hawaii and the South Sea Islands. We toured the West African coast, stopping at Mozambique and Kenya. At Cape Town, South Africa, we disembarked and were entertained by people we had already met on an earlier cruise.

We sailed up the Indian Ocean during the second cruise, to Dubai, and through the Red Sea, with stops in Aqaba, Jordan, and in Israel. In southern India, we disembarked at the port of Cochin, where we were greeted by a lineup of elephants in magnificent array and the head of the Jewish community. According to some historians, Jews came to Cochin after the destruction of the Temple in Jerusalem in 70 C.E. and again after the Spanish expulsion of 1492. We visited Cochin's ancient synagogue, the only Jewish site to be pictured on an Indian postage stamp. Sadly only fifteen to twenty Jewish families remain in Cochin today. Still, it has a place of honor in both Jewish and Indian history.

It was just before Passover when we reached Bombay. As Leonard disembarked, he struck up a conversation with the local representative of the shipping line. When he learned Leonard was a rabbi, he offered to arrange a meeting with Captain Sassoon, the head of the entire port of Bombay.

The Sassoons, of Baghdad origin and Vidal Sassoon fame, are one of the oldest and wealthiest Jewish families in India. They have been very philanthropic, building libraries, schools, and other institutions all over the country.

We were brought to Captain Sassoon's office. He was as handsome as a Hollywood star and very welcoming. At one point in our conversation, he noticed Leonard looking at his watch. "Do you have to go someplace?" he asked.

"My wife has an appointment on board to get her hair done," Leonard said.

"Oh, that is no problem," Captain Sassoon said. "I'll cancel that appointment and have my driver take you to our home. My wife will arrange for Mrs. Goldstein to go to her hairdresser."

We were driven to the Sassoon apartment. Over the lintel was a sign in Hebrew: "*Bruchim Habaim*" (welcome). In the living room was a recess that held a *Torah*. Mrs. Sassoon explained that the Progressive synagogue in Bombay (part of the international Reform movement) had burned down and its *Torah*s had been destroyed. She received this one as a replacement when she went to Thailand as a delegate to a convention of Progressive synagogues. "But since our synagogue had not yet been rebuilt," she explained, "I had to keep it in the house.

"Well, we could not just have it lying around. We needed a place to put it," she continued. "So we built an ark against the wall. And, of course, having a *Torah* in our home, we had to learn more about it. Until then, we had not been observant or knowledgeable. Now we felt we had to learn."

Then she excused herself for a moment and returned with a round *matzoh* she had baked. "Here is one thing I have learned," she said in the perfect British-style English spoken by Indians.

The Sassoons have three daughters. The youngest, a girl of about fourteen, had accompanied her mother to the convention and now was on fire to learn more about Judaism.

All through our travels, wherever we stopped, we looked for a Jewish community, a synagogue, or even a cemetery. And we were rarely disappointed. In Barbados we found a Jewish cemetery with tombstones that had skulls and bones. This mark often appears on Jewish graves in the

Caribbean although it has nothing to do with pirates. In Papeete, on Tahiti in the South Pacific, we found a modern synagogue as beautiful as a jewel box. In Malaysia we found a cemetery, evidence of a one-time Jewish community that has since relocated in Singapore. In Tunis we found a *Chabad* rabbi who had been living there for many years, serving the remnants of a once thriving population that has largely emigrated to France and Israel.

Our cruises have been extraordinary experiences. We have been to places most people only read about or see in movies, traveling in a style that can safely be described as imperial. We have met and have been befriended by people who hail from places as close to home as Trenton, New Jersey, and as distant as Auckland, New Zealand.

But for me, the deepest and most lasting pleasure of our cruising experience comes from the realization of the impact Leonard has had on so many people. They came on a cruise for a holiday. They were hardly observant, if at all. Yet I could see how their interest was sparked, how they began to contemplate the values of Judaism, and how they developed a curiosity about Jewish ritual. In so many cases, I had the feeling they would become more observant after they returned home. And more often than not, I was right. We've received so many letters telling us how Leonard's services and our example inspired them to enrich their Jewish lives. Not a consequence one would typically expect from taking a cruise.

Of all the rituals Leonard performed on board, the one I loved best was *Tashlich*. After services the first day of *Rosh Hashanah*, he would lead the congregants, all supplied with breadcrumbs, onto the deck and we would fling our crumbs into the sea, symbolically throwing away our sins. Being out on the ocean with no land in sight, with the sky vast and open before us and no one around but the soaring seagulls, we truly experienced the sense of awe the High Holy Days are meant to inspire.

Leonard would explain how the custom picked up the biblical verse of casting one's sins upon the waters. But at the same time, he would add, by using crumbs we were performing the charitable act of feeding the fish. Thus the spiritual purpose of the holy day was combined with an ecological one.

As he spoke, I would look around at those gathered for the ceremony. All were totally attentive, all seemingly moved. And what satisfaction I would take in knowing that this gentle pastor, who had brought me to the far corners of the world, was making so great a difference in so many lives.

XIII

COUNTING BLESSINGS

MANY A TIME I would begin a speech: "I bring you regards from 3080 Broadway, the Jewish Theological Seminary, where Jewish living and learning has been going on for decades." So strong is my attachment to this institution that I am driven to let the world know of it.

From within the Seminary walls, I have witnessed the changing position of American Jewry. My involvement began during the postwar years, when anti-Semitism, whether overt or discreet, restricted Jewish participation in many areas of society, and it continues into the present where the highest echelons of political, economic, cultural, and social life are open to Jews. Over this period, the Seminary has evolved into a major participant on the American academic playing field, having become a distinguished university in comfortable company with its neighbors: Columbia University and Barnard College. Undergraduates earn joint degrees, combining work at either of these schools with the Seminary's List College. Gentile as well as Jewish graduate students can pursue advanced degrees in Jewish law, philosophy, and history. Many go on to become professors of Jewish studies at the foremost universities of the United States and Israel. At the same time, the Seminary continues its initial mission and remains the premier American institution for the training of Conservative rabbis.

There were times when I would be out on the road speaking about the Seminary, and I would think back to the time I first heard of it as a young teenager spending *Shabbat* in my grandfather's house. Back then I pictured an exalted place, a castle up on a hill somewhere in the northern part of New York City. And I was not far from wrong.

But little did I dream that its gates would be thrown open to me, that I would get to know its workings, and that the great thinkers that comprised its faculty and administration would become my mentors and friends. In particular I am thinking of the three chancellors I knew and worked closely with: Louis Finkelstein, Gerson Cohen, and Ismar Schorsch, as well as eminent scholars like Abraham Heschel, who ironically seemed to exert more of an influence on Christian theologians across the street at the Union Theological Seminary than Jewish scholars on his own campus, and Mordecai Kaplan, the rabbi who introduced the concept of Judaism as a civilization and founded the Reconstructionist Movement.

I remember when Rabbi Finkelstein invited leading non-Jewish theologians to the Seminary, people on the order of Rienhold Niebuhr and Paul Tillich, to participate in interfaith dialogues. I remember when he took on Arnold Toynbee who compared civilizations to individuals, saying they are born, develop, and ultimately die. Because the Jewish civilization did not fit into his category, he dismissed it as a fossil. Rabbi Finkelstein invited Toynbee for dinner and a tour of the Seminary. After their evening together, the historian was suitably impressed and in a subsequent book, he apologized to the Jewish people. Nevertheless, as Rabbi Finkelstein noted, Toynbee's theory remains well known.

I was so taken with Chancellor Finkelstein, that whatever he said seemed correct to me at the time. He was against the Seminary becoming a university. He did not want a Seminary law school or medical school. "Let them go to Yeshiva University for that," he'd say. At the time, I thought he was right. Now I'm not so certain.

I had heard that Rabbi Finkelstein was originally not an avid Zionist. He felt the future of the Jewish people was here in the United States and not Israel, and he was very rigid in his thinking. Leonard told me that when he was graduating from the Seminary in 1948, he and his classmates requested that their commencement ceremony conclude with the singing of "*Hatikvah*" along with "*Adon Olam*" in honor of Israel's having just achieved statehood, but Dr. Finkelstein would not allow it.

The students went on strike, declaring they would not graduate if "*Hatikvah*" were not sung. Whereupon, Leonard said, Dr. Finkelstein called the class together and in his most persuasive manner convinced the young men to go along with his wishes.

The graduation was held on the Seminary quadrangle, and ended with the singing of "*Adon Olam*" as expected. Then, Leonard said, without warning, the bells of Riverside Church a block away began to peal out "*Hatikvah*," its soaring melody filling the air all around Morningside Heights. It was a thrilling moment, Leonard told me, and he never forgot it. But he never learned who arranged for it to happen or what Chancellor Finkelstein's reaction was.

All that was many years before my involvement. By the mid 1960s Rabbi Finkelstein was very much enamored with the Jewish State. I recall one speech where he declared the love of parents and grandparents for children is more visible in Israel than anyplace else, that it was the idea of Israel that sustained the Jews in the Diaspora and which accounts for its remarkable vitality.

Rabbi Finkelstein had retired, and Gerson Cohen was the new chancellor when the Seminary board voted in favor of allowing women to become rabbis. I know Rabbi Cohen was originally opposed to such a change, although he did come to accept it. I wonder whether Usher, who died shortly before the ruling, would have ever accepted it. I must confess, however, I am glad to see women play an active role in synagogue rituals that were closed to them merely a generation ago.

Lynn Liberman, a young woman who was an exceptional student in my Speech Preparation and Presence course at the Seminary, is now the rabbi of Knesses Israel Synagogue in Pittsfield, Massachusetts, where Leonard and I attend services whenever we are in Copake. Each time I am there, I am so taken by the enthusiasm and level of participation of her congregation, and my conviction is reinforced that there is no reason why women should not be rabbis. Today the debate has shifted to the issue of whether there should be gay Conservative rabbis, and once again, I find myself in the liberal wing.

It is ironic that while more women are taking an active role in Conservative synagogue life, fewer are involved in Women's League. Our current membership is far smaller than it was during my presidency. This development is a reflection of the larger scene, for as women enter professional life in greater numbers, the ranks of volunteers in the organizational world become thinner. Women's League has also been affected by demographic changes. I was so honored to serve as the first president of Brooklyn Branch. Sadly, it is no more. With the closing of many Conservative synagogues in the borough and a reduction in the membership of its sisterhoods, Brooklyn has once again been swallowed up, this time in the South Shore Long Island Branch.

Nevertheless, Women's League and the Seminary continue their partnership, one institution enhancing the other. The main synagogue of the Seminary, located in what used to be the reading room of the library, was built with over two million dollars raised by Women's League. The colorful *parochet* before its ark is my gift to this special place. It honors my three daughters-in-law: Susan and Janet, and Linda Kirshblum.

It has always been a source of satisfaction to sense the respect and esteem in which Women's League has been held by the Seminary leadership. I was very moved when Rabbi Schorsch described the value of our organization by referring to the *midrash* that deals with the period of rebellion in the wilderness, quoting the passage: "In that generation the women restored what the men destroyed."

But men restore as well. I am thinking in particular of Leonard Sharzer, a Seminary graduate who, as a plastic surgeon, had done more than his share of restoration. We met him on a cruise when he volunteered to recite the *kiddush* during Friday evening services. I was so taken with his beautiful voice that afterwards I asked his wife where he learned to recite the *kiddush* so well. "Oh, he will be graduating from the Jewish Theological Seminary in a few months," she said.

Her husband, the son of a doctor, had acceded to his father's wishes and become a physician, she told me. Five years earlier, he decided to change careers and has been studying at the Seminary ever since.

Not long ago, Rabbi Leonard and Lois Sharzer invited us to a *Shabbat* dinner at their country home near Copake, where they sang the entire Friday night services the way they do at B'nai Jeshurun Synagogue on the Upper West Side. That was when we learned Leonard Sharzer was encouraged to study for the rabbinate by B'nai Jeshurun's rabbi, J. Rolando Matalon, who inherited the pulpit from the late Marshall Meyer. In such ways are my connections to the Seminary continued and reinforced.

Although neither Al Fried nor Usher left me a great deal of money, I was able to continue the habit of my very young years of squirreling much of my earnings away. A few years ago, when I discovered just how much I had squirreled away, I was bowled over. I said to myself, my children are all very well off. If I leave my money to my sons, they'll just give it to their Orthodox causes. I don't want the money I worked so hard for going to any causes other than the ones I support: Open University of Israel, Women's League, the Jewish Braille Institute, and, most importantly, the Seminary.

Then Leonard suggested that instead of donating a lump sum of money to the Seminary, I endow a chair that would insure the kind of work I had done would continue. It seemed a wonderful idea. And that was how the Helen Fried Kirshblum Goldstein Chair of Practical Rabbinics came to be.

The banquet honoring the establishment of this chair was held in the library building. It was a glittering event. Many guests wandered up to the mezzanine level, where some of the rare books are displayed, and as I looked about the splendid building on that splendid evening, I was reminded of an afternoon more than thirty years ago when I was driving home on the West Side Highway and heard on the radio that part of the Seminary was on fire. Immediately, I turned around and drove back in a fury, only to park my car across the street and watch the flames consume the library tower. My tears flowed like the water from the firemen's hoses.

The next morning I assembled a group of women, and we spent days blotting and re-leafing rescued books with paper towels. After that, Women's League worked very hard raising funds to refurbish the library. What a beautiful, state-of-the-art building it is today, I thought, and how appropriate a place to celebrate the endowment of a chair that tied together two major strands of my life: my profession as a teacher of speech and my passion for Judaism.

That night was a high point in my life. I felt blessed indeed with my marriage, my children and grandchildren, rewarded by a life filled with charitable activities and punctuated by cruises to exotic ports of call. Then suddenly things took a sudden turn for the worse.

I found that inexplicably I was losing my balance. More and more frequently I would fall to the ground for no obvious reason. My condition was diagnosed as hydrocephalus, what my mother used to call "water on the brain." To release the accumulated water, I was told, a shunt was needed to be installed under the skin from the brain to the abdomen.

It was one of those cases where the operation was a success, but the patient nearly died. After coming out of the anesthesia, I suffered a severe stroke. For days, I lay in a coma. Arthur flew in from Israel. Everyone thought it was the end.

This was not the first time I suffered a stroke. Years before, when I was married to Usher, I was sitting at my desk one morning feeling perfectly fine, when all of a sudden I was unable to speak. I threw a book down the stairs to get Usher's attention. By the time he ran upstairs, my speech was garbled, and soon afterwards I was speaking normally again. A mini stroke is that quick.

I think Usher was more frightened than I. He must have been reminded of one of Selma's epileptic spells. At the time, we were all set to leave for a mission to Jerusalem with the congregation, and I certainly didn't want Usher to miss it. Fortunately Dr. Jacoby told us it had passed. His neurologist colleague at Mount Sinai concurred. We went on the trip and all was fine.

But there was the memory of that trauma. Speech was my field. How can I live without speaking, I would think. "Horror, horror, horror!" I had written in my book when it happened. That mini stroke was my first indication of mortality. I had never been sick before.

I was married to Leonard when I suffered a second mini stroke, a third, and then a fourth. By then I had had the experience, had spoken to other people about it, and knew I would get better quickly. But this was a major stroke and of an entirely different order.

Finally, I came out of my coma but had to spend weeks in the hospital before being transferred to the Rusk Institute, an excellent rehabilitation center associated with NYU. During the next month I learned to walk and talk again. The director, Dr. Jung Ahn, my therapist Dr. Judith Leventhal, and the entire Rusk staff were enormously kind and competent, interested in the welfare of the patients. And I was a model patient, determined to do everything I could to get well. I kept feeling, I'm getting better, I'm getting better, I'm getting better.

Dr. Leventhal had me bring in some photos to jolt my long-term memory; she encouraged me to do a lot of talking about the events they suggested. Every time I did this, a piece of the past came rushing back.

After a while I felt I no longer had to attend the group sessions that were part of my therapy. Why should I take someone's place, I thought. But then I realized my experience as a speech professor was enabling me to lead the direction of the group, to introduce ideas and techniques. For example, I came up with the concept of our introducing one another based on little interviews each person would perform with the person to his or her right. We'd write down the answers to the questions we posed. The professional on hand would help those who could not write. It not only gave each of us a speaking experience but also practice in remembering. And it struck me how even at this point in my life, I was reaping the benefits of teaching, being rewarded for providing a service to others.

Some time after my discharge, I received a call from Eric Heffler, executive director of American Friends of Open University. Five women, including myself, were going to be honored as "Women of Leadership and Vision" at a dinner given at the new downtown Marriott, and the organizers wanted me to accept the award on behalf of us all.

I hesitated. Since my stroke, I had not spoken in public. Also I wondered how the other women would feel about my speaking for them. "Maybe each of us should make a brief statement," I said to Eric. But he was insistent that I be the sole speaker.

It was very difficult for me. But I was determined. And I did it centering my talk on the stories of some Open University graduates whose lives were transformed through their connection with that institution.

The evening was but another outstanding event in a life of many outstanding events. But perhaps none was a more complete and joyous coming together than my ninetieth birthday party.

Whenever the subject of my age came up, I would say, "Age is just a number and I'm unlisted." My attitude was like President Clinton's formula for gays in the military: "Don't ask, don't tell." But as I approached my ninetieth birthday, I felt reaching such an age was something worth marking, and so, unlike Dan Goldstein, when my children told me they wanted to give me a party, I readily agreed.

Michael made all the arrangements for a Sunday morning brunch at Shallots. About 130 people were invited, and as they arrived in the flower-filled, balloon-decked restaurant, there he was, the garrulous host, welcoming everyone, and spontaneously organizing who should sit with whom.

Each guest inspired special reflections, cherished memories. I saw Mim and Saul Teplitz and thought of the many Women's League programs Mim and I had worked on together through the years, and how Saul had been the rabbi who married not only my children but also Leonard and me. When Joseph and Linda Kastner, friends of Michael and Janet's who became my friends as well, came into the restaurant, I was reminded of the time years ago when Linda was reluctant to have a baby since Joseph already had three children from a previous marriage, and how emphatic I had been in persuading her not to go through life without having a child of her own. Ultimately I convinced her. And every time I see Zohar, a spirited young man who is now a student at Bar Ilan University in Israel, I feel I am part of him.

The Seminary was represented by Vice Chancellor William Lebeau and his wife, Beverly, and Chancellor Ismar Schorsch and his wife, Sally. How honored I was by their presence. Of all the Seminary chancellors I've known, I've had the closest relationship with Ismar Schorsch. I admire him as a scholar and as a leader. I also cherish him as a dear friend.

And then there was family. For me, family has always been top priority. I had kept the connections going through the decades of my life. And this day, I was rewarded by having every clan – from the Feiners to the Boehms to the Frieds to the Kirshblums to the Goldsteins – represented. As I greeted each relation, it was as if my life, like the reels of an old movie, was rolling before my eyes.

When my niece Ellen and her partner, Joan Starkman, walked in, my mind flashed back to the morning my sister called me crying hysterically. "I have such bad news. It's Ellen."

I thought she was pregnant. "Don't worry, Nettie," I told her. "We'll get her an abortion. No one has to know about it."

"Are you kidding?" she cried. "I only wish she were pregnant. She's a lesbian."

Sam Feldman had great difficulty acknowledging his daughter's homosexuality. But Nettie soon got used to the idea and treated it with her typical sense of humor. "Okay, you're gay," she'd say to Ellen. "I accept it. But why can't you at least be with a Jewish girl?"

If she were alive, how happy Nettie would be to know that today Ellen lives with a fine Jewish woman and her son. Ellen is a teacher. Like her mother, she's an expert golfer, and she's leading a happy and fulfilled life.

Ellen was an only child. But Hy and Millicent had two children: Dickie, who was not able to attend, and Victoria who happily was.

Of all her grandchildren, I think my mother favored Vicki the most.

She would carry on, in front of Arthur and Michael, about how brilliant and beautiful, and talented Vicki was. I know they would get annoyed. Truthfully there were times I would get annoyed too. But then again, Vicki has always been brilliant, beautiful, and talented.

She graduated from Vassar and was an accomplished pianist. Then, at the age of twenty-three, she lost the sight of her right eye, and a promising performing career was cut short. Nevertheless, she had a good life with her husband, Eugene Roth, a hematologist at Mount Sinai, and their son Marco, until some time in the 1990s, when tragically Eugene contracted AIDS from an infected patient and subsequently died.

Now I greeted Vicki, who looked as lovely as ever. She told me her mother was doing well in a nursing home in the Philadelphia area. Hy had died some years ago, and seeing Vicki brought back memories of my big brother who had been such a great athlete in his time, even playing football for NYU. He graduated in 1938 during the depths of the Depression but he managed to get a job through the NRA (National Recovery Administration) before moving on to a long and successful career as an industrial engineer. Hy and Millicent lived in Pennsylvania most of their married lives. Nevertheless, our relationship remained strong through the years.

My half sister, Chaneleh, and her husband, Joe Kleiner, had been dear to me, and I was sorry that their children, Howard, Gloria, and Dan, were unable to attend the party. But Gloria's son, Dr. Perry Eisman came. A researcher for Pfizer, Perry had called me one day to see if I could help him research the Feiner family history, and we have stayed in touch ever since.

How delighted I was to welcome Howard Boehm and his wife Isabelle. The son of my Uncle Sam, who together with my grandfather had founded the Philosophical Press, Howard has been my good friend as well as my cousin since we were kids. He's an optometrist, and not only has he taken good care of my eyes through the years, he's also consistently kept me in the most fashionable glasses. When I was first suggested to Usher as a woman he might want to meet, a congregant warned him, "I don't think you can afford her. She owns a different pair of glasses to go with every outfit."

Al Fried's family was represented by his sister Ida's son, Sandy Posner, who had been like my own child through all his growing up years. Sandy's entire family came along: his wife, Susan, their three sons and daughters-in-law and grandchild. One of their sons, Dr. Mark Posner, and his wife, Debbie, had flown in from Chicago to join my celebration.

But they were not the only ones to travel great distances. Eliezer and Linda Kirshblum with daughter Risa and son Jonathan came down from Toronto. Their daughter Shari came all the way from Tel Aviv with her baby son, and Eliezer's sister, Marsha, and her husband, Larry Wachsman, came all the way from Jerusalem. Seeing how well-suited Marsha and Larry are to one another, I thought for the thousandth time what a pity it was that Usher did not live to see his daughter married to such a fine man. But I also remembered how good I had felt to make Marsha's wedding and walk her down the aisle.

Marsha and Larry are very close to Arthur and Susan who, naturally, were there to celebrate my ninetieth with the entire clan, except for Elisheva, my youngest and very affectionate granddaughter, who was in the army's intelligence corps and was not allowed to leave the country.

I drank in all my other Israeli grandchildren, the five girls and the one boy, Avi, who has legally changed his name to Albert (although everyone still calls him Avi). When I notice his natural elegance and many kindnesses, especially the respect he shows to older people, I see in him the first love of my life.

Avi and his wife, Merav, a marketer in the television industry, live a secular lifestyle in Tel Aviv. I had wondered what Arthur's reaction would be to Avi's giving up Orthodox observance. After all, this is his only son, the only one to carry on the family name. But apparently Arthur has accepted Avi's way of life as well as that of Sara and her husband Micah Avni, who, like his brother-in-law, works in the financial realm.

From the time she was a little girl, Sara was always the one to sit on one side of her father on Friday nights and holidays (Avi, of course, would be on the other). This day I looked at her admiringly. How elegant she is, so tall, slender and well put together. Independent, a bit of a rebel, Sara practiced law for a while, and then decided it was not for her. She went back to school and reinvented herself as a high school teacher, a profession she enjoys greatly.

Debra married her childhood sweetheart, David Bernstein, a student at Bar Ilan University. Seeing her brimming with life and energy, I thought of how the others used to make fun of her because she was not as scholastically inclined as they. Debra may not have gone to Hebrew University like they did, but she does attend the Bezalel Academy of Art, one of the world's premier schools of fine art. When it comes to artistic talent, Debra outshines them all.

Abigail, who encouraged me to buy the diamond pin I coveted, is married to Eyal Haimovsky, an assistant to the Mayor of Jerusalem. She is an occupational therapist, and as I watched her easy interaction with the other guests, it was clear that her natural sense of warmth and patience enables her to do so much good for the disabled people with whom she works.

When I saw Zippy, whose girlhood awkwardness was once my concern, moving gracefully among the crowd, I realized how foolish my worries had been. She's an executive recruiter today, charming, extroverted, and married to Micah Goodman, a teacher who appears on Israeli television every Friday discussing the *Torah* portion of the week.

But of all the grandchildren, everyone was flocking around my first grandchild, Alissa, and her husband, Rabbi David Harbater, to sneak a peek at my first great-grandchildren, Ayelet and Yael. Alissa was positively glowing this day in her young motherhood.

As exciting as it was to have nearly all the Israeli branch of the family gathered together in New York on this special day, I drew equal pleasure from the sight of my two local granddaughters who, because they live in New York, have been part of my life from the minute they were born. In my mind's eye, I pictured them as little girls spending *Shabbat* in Kew Garden Hills, running up to the *bimah* to be scooped up in Usher's arms, dressing up in my clothes and performing made-up plays on the living room steps. I thought of all the special times in their lives that I had shared, the birthday parties, bat mitzvahs, and graduations, and how I had watched them grow from high-spirited kids into the lovely young women they are today.

Rachel, married to Nimrod Dayan, a warm and giving pediatrician, had studied communications at the University of Maryland. She worked for NBC but would go on to do public relations work for her father at Shallots. Miriam was hitting her stride at her father's alma mater Brooklyn Law School. Soon she'd graduate and join an excellent law firm.

And then, of course, I had to take note of my sons and their wives. How much *naches* they had given me through the years, what exceptional people they are. Of late, Michael had played a leading role in the renovation of his synagogue, *Orach Chaim* on Manhattan's Upper East Side. Arthur was now heading *Avi Chai* (My Father Lives), the foundation endowed by the late Sanford (Zalman) Bernstein, in fulfillment of the pledge Arthur had made to the financier/philanthropist.

It gives me special satisfaction to know that among the principal missions of *Avi Chai* is the furthering of Jewish day schools throughout the world. Nearly forty years ago, I had spoken at a United Synagogue board meeting to argue in favor of a resolution that would sponsor Conservative day schools in America. They were not common then and enjoyed little public support. But my involvement in Women's League had led me to understand how important they are for the furtherance of quality Jewish education, and I spoke strongly in favor of the resolution. It was adopted, but by a narrow vote. A few years later, history repeated itself at a board meeting of Women's League. Again I argued with some vehemence in favor of a similar resolution. Again it narrowly passed. How fitting it now seemed that my son was heading a philanthropic organization with great resources, which wholeheartedly supported the once fledgling movement I had promoted many years ago.

When Arthur assumed his position at *Avi Chai*, he was obligated to leave the Rothschild Foundation. And they were most unhappy to see him go. There was no unhappiness this day however. With Leonard beside me, I looked out at a crowd illuminated by the many candles on my birthday cake. Every person there was dear to me. There were others, not visible, but whose presence was equally felt: my parents and grandparents, my sister and brother, my first love Al Fried, dearest Usher.

What a ride it had been for the little girl from Port Chester, New York, who from the time she sneaked into her brother's kindergarten class knew her seat would have to be always up front.

EPILOGUE

IN THE EARLY SPRING OF 2003, my sister-in-law Millicent died at the age of ninety-three. Leonard and I paid Vicki a *shiva* call at her apartment on West End Avenue. Her son, Marco, and his wife, Emily, were there as well, and Vicki invited us all into her dining room for tea. I walked in, looked at the beautifully-set table, and a wave of emotion swept over me. "What is it, Aunt Helen?" Vicki asked, seeing my eyes fill with tears.

"It's the tablecloth, dear," I said fingering the fabric, soft with age. "I remember when your mother embroidered it."

And then I told Vicki how before either of us was married, Millicent and I went out one day and bought tablecloths that had the outline of a wintry scene: sleighs and reindeer and people dressed in mufflers and furry hats. Hers was white, mine was off-white. Millicent had embroidered this tablecloth before us in blue thread while I had embroidered mine in a galaxy of colors.

Of course, Millicent would give her tablecloth to Vicki, just as I had given mine to Susan, who used it until it became worn. Then she cut it into pieces, had each segment framed, and distributed them among the children, Janet, and me.

The tablecloth brought back so many memories of Millicent. I thought of how Nettie and I had encouraged Hy to marry her, and how she had drawn the pattern for my wedding gown. I kept that gown until I was ready to move from the house in Kew Garden Hills.

My friend Charlotte came in the day of the tag sale and saw it hanging with other articles of clothing. "What are you doing with your wedding gown?" she asked.

"I'll either sell it or just give it to someone who'll appreciate it."

"No, you can't do that," Charlotte said. "I'll be going to Israel in a few weeks. Let me bring it to the girls."

As soon as Charlotte came into the house in Jerusalem, the children all came running. They not only loved Charlotte, they could always count on her to bring them terrific presents. "I have something special for you," she now said, opening a big box. "This is Nanny's wedding dress."

They laughed. "Nanny was never thin enough to get into that." But every one of the girls had to try it on, and they had a lot of fun with it.

Not long ago, Susan took the dress, freshened it up, and brought it to the costume department of a museum. Today, my wedding gown, mounted and framed, hangs in Arthur and Susan's bedroom.

That's Susan. An old tablecloth and an old wedding gown – those are the kinds of things that have meaning for her. Although she can well afford to buy whatever she likes, she seldom wears jewelry – except for the diamond brooch left to her by Lady Rothschild. And I know it is not the diamonds but the memory of the person that makes it valuable to her.

The last time Susan visited me in New York, I told her I wanted her to have something from my home. There were paintings, silver, antiques. She could have anything she liked. All she wanted was a *mezuzah*.

When I told Arthur I would be leaving my estate to my favorite causes, I asked him whether there was something from our life together that he would like to have. He looked around and looked around. "That picture of Grandma and Grandpa," he said finally. "I'd like that."

"Anything else?"

"No, Mother, there is nothing else."

Then I spoke to Michael, who is lighter hearted, but in his kibitzing, there is always some truth.

"I think that's very nice Mother," he said, when I told him about my bequests.

I said, "Look around. Is there anything you would like that would be a memento of our living together?"

And he said, "I'd like the old black photo album with photos of Grandma and Grandpa on the deck of the *Bremen* when they went to Europe."

I remember when Mama and Papa took that trip. At that time, the prospect of going abroad seemed so thrilling. I wondered if I would ever get to Europe. The idea of my seeing South America, Asia, Australia, and Africa never even occurred to me.

As things turned out, I've seen more than a few wonders of the world. I've been to the Taj Mahal, the ancient ruins of Greece and Rome, and the Great Barrier Reef. And yet, as I look back on my life, the places dearest to me are none of these. They won't be found in any guidebook. Still, they have a special place in my heart.

All through the years I taught at Kingsborough Community College, I drove past Temple Beth El in Manhattan Beach more times than I can remember. However, the first time I saw that synagogue was before the campus was even on the drawing boards. I was attending my first Women's League branch meeting, overwhelmed at the scope of the organization and the quality of the women I met. It was at Temple Beth El that I began my quest for learning, attending lectures and courses given by the incomparable Rabbi Morris Margolies. Later on Michael and Janet would be married at this same synagogue, and later still, Leonard would accept a pulpit there and move into the neighborhood, triggering the chain of events that would lead to our coming together.

Decades later, after Leonard and I were married, I would drive to Kingsborough from Manhattan, going down the East River Drive, crossing the Brooklyn Bridge and taking the Belt Parkway to the Sheepshead Bay exit. One day, on an impulse, I got off at the Bay Ridge exit instead. I had a yen to visit my grandfather's synagogue.

I was taken aback for the moment not to see Isaac Boehm's portrait hanging in the vestibule before quickly reminding myself this building had ceased being a synagogue in the 1960s, when B'nai Israel was sold to a Protestant church. Then I entered the sanctuary, took a seat in one of the pews, and looked up at the Tiffany-like stained glass windows. And for a moment, it was as if nothing had changed. I thought of the impact this place had had on my life, how it was the vehicle through which I was first exposed to Conservative Judaism as a young teenager; how it was at the B'nai Israel Sunday School that I first tried my hand at teaching many, many years ago.

Peter Cooper Village, the apartment complex right off the East River Drive, is where Michael and Janet began their married life together. In one of the strange twists of fate, Rachel and Nimrod moved into the exact same apartment when they got married. Their baby and my third great-grand-child, Rebecca Rose (whom I call the "Centerpiece"), gets wheeled in her stroller up and down the same pathways Janet once wheeled Rachel.

One day, on my way home from Kingsborough, I stopped to visit Rachel and Nimrod, and sitting in their living room, I casually glanced out the window. I must have looked out that same window countless times in the past. But now, for the first time, I noticed the public baths across the way. Somehow I'd never noticed them before. And suddenly it dawned on me those were the public baths I used to see when I looked out the window of Auto Truck Garage. Peter Cooper Village had to have been built on the very site of the office and garage where I had finagled my way into getting hired as a bookkeeper more than sixty years before.

A few years ago, a neighbor in Copake, Jay Rosenblatt, asked Leonard if he would marry him to his fiancée, Pat. The wedding took place in the exquisite apartment of Pat's close friend, Mira Van Doren of the famous scholarly Van Doren family, in a building they owned on West Fifty-seventh Street in New York City.

Both Mira and her husband, John, were very taken with Leonard. "When my mother dies, I want Rabbi Goldstein to do the service," Mira told John.

Mira's mother, Lydia, died the summer of 2003 at the age of ninety-five, and Leonard was asked to officiate. At the chapel, the various elements of her life were on display. There were samples of her work as a fashion designer and toy manufacturer, her artwork, and photographs of her dating back to her early childhood in Vilna.

One of Mira's grandsons recited the *kaddish* at the gravesite. Although John Van Doren is not Jewish, his and Mira's children were raised Jewishly. The renowned Van Doren line now has a Jewish branch.

After the burial, we all assembled in John and Mira's apartment. We'd visited before, and each time, Lydia would come down from her apartment in the same building with her companion. I always approached her, spoke with her. She was so very charming, so very warm.

A talented singer and guitarist from the Ukraine who often entertains at Mira's parties was there this day performing some melancholy Yiddish and Russian songs. The traditional part of me was saying disapprovingly,

"Singing? At a house of *shiva*?" But the rest of me was saying, "It is so beautiful, so apropos."

After a while, the singer paused and left the room for a few moments. Then she returned, picked up her guitar, and began to sing "*Ich hob dir tsoo feel lieb tsoo zein oif dir in kas*" – "I love you much too much to be angry with you."

I was stunned. This was the old Yiddish song my father would sing to me when I was a little girl. A powerful sense of yearning and nostalgia flowed through me, and although it had been decades since I last heard the lyrics, every word came back to me. I sang along quietly as if I were a child again bathed in the glow of my beloved father. And at that moment, it seemed to me that my entire life had come full circle.

I live the day and do the day. I look ahead, not behind. Every once in a while I think of death. But I brush it out of my mind. I don't want to think that way at all. I want to think I'm going to go on and on and on. And when the day comes that I can't, I want to just close my eyes…

Helen did close her eyes early in the morning of January 4, 2004. On a cruise with her beloved Leonard, she was saying goodbye to some friends before entering the port of San Juan, Puerto Rico, failed to notice a step behind her, and suffered the fall which led to her death the following week.

Sadly she has not lived to see the publication of these memoirs. But in large part, Helen's last year on earth was spent in full possession of her faculties and with the wisdom of her many years, recalling, recounting, and reflecting upon the events of her well-lived life. This book is the result of that process; its creation is, in itself, a gift to us all – a testament and a blessing.

GLOSSARY

The definitions below explain the Hebrew and Yiddish (Y.) terms used in this book. Sometimes there are alternate spellings and definitions for these words. Here the spelling and definitions reflect the way the terms are used in this book.

Adon Olam: A liturgical hymn, proclaiming the Lord's providence.

Aishet Chayil: A woman of valor; an upright, God-fearing woman.

aliyah: (1) Returning from the Diaspora to live in Israel. (2) (pl. *aliyot*) The honor of being called up to read blessings over the *Torah*.

Ashkenazi (adj. Ashkenazic): A Jew of German or Eastern European descent.

Av Hayishuv: Father of the Settlement. The name given to Baron Edmond de Rothschild.

bikkur cholim: The charitable act of visiting the sick.

bimah: A platform in the center of the synagogue upon which the Torah is read.

Bruchim Habaim: Literally: the comers are blessed; a salutation of welcome.

Chabad: The acronym for *Chochma, Bina, Da'at*; another name for the *Lubavitch chassidic* sect.

chai: Life; the Hebrew letters whose combined numerical equivalent is eighteen.

challah: The braided egg bread used on the Sabbath.

chassid: A member of a *chassidic* sect, often distinguished by Old World dress, devotion to a *rebbe*, and emotional religiosity.

cholent: (Y.) A dish made of beans and beef that simmers in the oven from Friday afternoon through sundown Saturday.

chuppah: A wedding canopy.

daven: (Y.) Pray.

d'var Torah: A brief discourse on a *Torah*-related topic.

farbissina: (Y.) One with a bitter personality.

farbringens: (Y.) Get-togethers of the *Chassidim*.

gabbai: A synagogue official who oversees the proceedings of services as well as holding various other congregational responsibilities.

get: A Jewish ritual divorce.

Haggadot: Plural of *Haggadah* – a printed account of the Exodus with accompanying songs and prayers, used at the Passover *seder*; literally: recitation.

halachic: According to Jewish law.

Hatikvah: Israel's national anthem.

havdalah: A ceremony that marks the end of the Sabbath and holidays.

Hohekreisch: (Y.) A naming ceremony for a baby girl.

kaddish: The memorial prayer.

ketubah: A marriage contract.

kibbutz: A collective agricultural settlement unique to Israel.

kiddush: Prayers and accompanying ceremony that sanctify the Sabbath and holy days.

Knesset: Israel's house of parliament.

kochalayan: (Y.) A vacation boardinghouse where each family had its own cooking privileges.

kugel: (Y.) A pudding usually made with potatoes or noodles.

Lubavitch: See *Chabad*.

Lubavitcher: A member of the *Lubavitch chassidic* sect.

Lubavitcher Rebbe: The leader of the *Lubavitcher* sect.

marit ayin: How it looks to the eye; relating to an act that may appear to be one that is prohibited in Jewish law, even though it may not be under certain circumstances.

matzoh: Unleavened bread eaten during Passover.

Megillah: A scroll, story; particularly the story of Queen Esther's saving of the Jews of Persia read on *Purim*.

meshuggina: (Y.) Crazy person.

mezuzah: An oblong-shaped casing containing verses from Deuteronomy that is hung on a doorpost.

midrash: One or a collection of rabbinic interpretations of the Bible.

mikveh: A ritual bath.

mincha: The afternoon prayer service.

minyan: A quorum of ten required for public prayer.

mitzvah: A meritorious act; a commandment; one of 613 *mitzvot* (pl.) of the *Torah*.

naches: (Y.) Pride, especially from one's children.

neshama: Soul.

oleh: One who settles in Israel.

parochet: The curtain that covers the ark in the synagogue.

Pesach: Passover.

Purim: The holiday celebrating Queen Esther's saving of the Jews in Persia, usually marked by elaborate festivities.

rebbe: (Y.) The leader of a *chassidic* sect.

rebbetzen: (Y.) The wife of a rabbi.

Rosh Hashanah: The Jewish new year.

seder (pl. *sedarim*): The festive banquet held the first two nights of Passover accompanied by the reading of the *Haggadah*; literally: order.

seudah: A banquet.

Sephardi (adj. Sephardic): A Jew of Spanish or Portuguese descent.

Shehecheyanu: The prayer of thanksgiving.

Shabbat: Sabbath.

Shabbat Shalom: Greetings on the Sabbath.

Shabbos: (Y.) Sabbath.

shiksa: (Y.) A gentile girl.

shiva: The seven-day period of mourning.

Shema: The prayer affirming monotheism.

shticklach: (Y.) A mannerism that can be endearing or affected.

shul: (Y.) Synagogue.

siddur: A prayer book.

sukkah: An outdoor tent-like eating area used during *Sukkoth*.

Sukkoth: The eight-day harvest festival.

tallit: A prayer shawl.

Talmud Torah: Hebrew school held after regular school hours.

Tashlich: The ceremony of symbolically casting one's sins into water on the first day of *Rosh Hashanah*, customarily using breadcrumbs to represent sins.

Tikkun Olam: The repair of the world.

Torah: A handwritten scroll containing the five books of Moses.

tsuris: (Y.) Trouble.

tzedakah: Charity.

Yahrtzeit: (Y.) The yearly commemoration of a family member's death.

yarmulke: (Y.) A skull cap.

Yiddishkeit: (Y.) The essence of Eastern European Yiddish culture.

z"l: May their memories be for a blessing.

INDEX